'AULD BOB'
A man in a million

**Edited by
Mary Docherty**

Copies of this book may be obtained from the following:
Bob Selkirk (Junior) 89 Union Street, Cowdenbeath, Fife.
Jack Allen, 70 Selkirk Avenue Cowdenbeath, Fife

Printed by Lancashire Community Press (TU), 8 Higher Bank Road, Preston PR2

CONTENTS

ACKNOWLEDGEMENTS

I wish to thank Wullie Braid, Alex Maxwell and W. Anderson for their testimonies to Bob included in this book.

My special thanks to Irene Gallacher, Wullie Braid, Susan Galloway and Lyn and Jim Hammonds for their continued help and encouragement.

"Auld Bob"

BOB SELKIRK

Bob Selkirk was a household word in our house in the early 1940s, and in those days it was a brave man that openly called himself a spokesman for the working class, but to add you were a communist was a sure recipe for the establishment to make your life a misery. To encourage people to fight for their rights Bob produced many mining papers, i.e. 'The Lamp', 'Pan Bolt', 'Mash' and 'The Crawpicker'. In those early years they did not just refuse you employment, they put you in jail. Bob Selkirk found himself in the dock eight times and in jail twice. This type of treatment only made Bob more determined to fight injustice with all the determination of a trapped animal fighting for survival.

My father Jimmy Braid used to tell the miners in our area that Bob Selkirk, the miner who came to Fife prior to the 1926 Miners Strike would someday be a member of parliament, but Bob was too busy fighting for the common five eight and too humble to accept being nominated for this type of exalted position. He needed to walk the High Street and hear the peoples' grievances firsthand.

Mary Docherty, the author of this memorial to Bob Selkirk, is a living example of the teaching and principles of her friend and philosopher Bob Selkirk. Both Bob and Mary have written books about working class life and within the pages the reader can feel how hard these wonderful people built up a camaraderie between themselves and overcame adversity. We must never forget the people that perished, the wives and children that suffered and feel pride when we think of the Bob Selkirks of this world who gave their lives in the true sense of the word for our class, the working class, or as Bob would say, 'The Common Five Eight'.

Wullie Braid

PREFACE

Those who see the emancipation of the working class through a philosophy of collectivism and mass organisation frown on the "personality cult", whereby history is create by a "great man or woman". But working-class struggles, weaved around the experiences of one worker and the fellow workers, comrades, neighbours he or she associated with in a geographical locality, focuses on the true nature of working-class struggle. The poverty, the comradeship, the organisation, the victimisation by employers, the internationalist solidarity, the community politics of the mining community of Cowdenbeath in Fife are well demonstrated in this book.

Mary Docherty combines here her own recollections with the collected writings and experiences of Bob Selkirk to put on record the contribution of a mining community that elected and supported Communist representatives to their local Council and a Communist M.P. to Parliament.

INTRODUCTION

I thought it would be a shame not to write more of the life of Bob Selkirk. He could not include many of his experiences in his autobiography 'THE LIFE OF A WORKER' because of lack of money to print a longer book. I have added here my own and others' knowledge of the good work he did for the people of Fife, together with other pieces he left in the hope that some day they would be printed.

Bob's name was a household name in Cowdenbeath and further afield. Anybody with grievance or any difficulty concerning housing, debts, wife beatings, unfaithfulness, pensions, unemployment benefit, compensation – anything and everything – he gave them the best advice he could and never turned anyone away. Most of all, everyone knew that everything would be kept confidential.

'Auld Bob', as he was affectionately known, had many disappointments and set-backs, but in spite of them he never let go. He was known to everybody in Cowdenbeath and I am sure there was hardly a family he had not helped in some way or another. He kept on fighting and tried to get his points of view across to as many people as possible, believing that the pen is mightier than the sword. Many of his writings are included in the following chapters.

The full text of Bob's booklet 'THE LIFE OF A WORKER' is incorporated in this book, together with additional material he wrote and contributions by myself and others who worked, fought and campaigned with him for a Socialist society.

I am sure after reading this book you will agree with me that his life's work should be remembered as part of the history of working class struggle. Professor Matkovsky was right when he said Bob Selkirk was "A true son of the working class".

Mary Docherty, 1996

BOB SELKIRK

4

PART ONE

CHAPTER ONE
RECOLLECTIONS BY MARY DOCHERTY

Here's to him in pride bedecked
Full conscious of his class respect
Who lifts his head and stands erect
To stem corruptions tide

Who fights the tyrants of his race
Nor gold nor flattery can debase
With truth upon his fearless face
And justice by his side

I first met Bob Selkirk at a Public Meeting in 1926 in Cowdenbeath Co-operative Hall where, at the end of the meeting, he asked for people to join the Communist Party. I joined with a friend who was with me. Bob invited us to a training class to be held the next night, which we both enjoyed. He was never reluctant to pass on any information when asked and never looked on any other person as a likely rival to himself in the Communist Party. A shy man, on social occasions he tried to keep in the background. In politics he was as solid as a rock and fought hard for what he was fighting for. He was very well known as far afield as the Soviet Union, where he appeared more than once on television and was written about in Soviet newspapers.

One of the 'Pravda' reporters visited him all the way from Moscow for an interview, which is reprinted in this book (see pages 41–90). Another writer (Professor Matkovsky) wrote a book about Harry Pollitt, the National Secretary of the Communist Party, which he dedicated to Bob Selkirk, referring to him as "a true son of the working class".

He was a very honest person, a man of integrity who fought for what he was entitled to but never took what was not his. He always took a principled stand. Unlike some of the Tory MPs and Tory Cabinet Ministers who use their positions in the Government to seek high paid part-time jobs, he would never use his position for anything for his family or himself as a result of being a Councillor. For instance, when attending Fife County Council meetings in Cupar every month, he got his travelling expenses and lunch allowance. If he got a lift in someone's car instead of the bus, he always refused to take the bus allowance, in spite of the cashier always insisting that he should take it, saying "... take it Bob, all the others take it, even though they got a lift in a car". Bob always said he was only entitled to the lunch money.

He treated people's generosity in the same principled way. If anyone insisted on giving him money for doing something for them, he would give it to the treasurer of the Communist Party and ask him to send a receipt to the person for the money. The money would then be sent to the Party paper the 'Daily Worker' (later the 'Morning Star') or left to pay the rent of the Party rooms.

He never fell for the subtle forms of corruption prevalent in local and national government, a good example being the annual Summer day trip of the Town Council and some of its employees to 'inspect' the Town's reservoir. It cost a lot of money for this one day at the Ratepayers' expense, and it did not take long to inspect the reservoir.

This was always a sore spot with the Ratepayers with it costing so much money. Bob was determined that he was going to see that less money would have to be spent on this day out at the Ratepayers' expense. I don't think he went on the first one and he tried to find out, unsuccessfully, how much it cost. He and Dave Fairley went on it the next year to find out more about it.

They left by bus early and stopped at a hotel for breakfast; had refreshment at 11.00am; lunch at mid-day in another hotel; refreshments again in the afternoon, then dinner in the evening. All that to eat and drink as well as the tour by bus to parts of the north of Scotland. The reservoir was visited in the forenoon, which only took a short time before the bus tour took over. Drink and extras were also supplied. It cost hundreds of pounds, so Bob and Davie raised it in the Council, but of course, they did not get any support.

Bob never gave up, because he knew what the day was like. He let the Ratepayers know the full details so that they could let the Councillors know what they felt about it and support his criticisms. In time he did get the cost cut down. In future years they did not start so early and instead of going to hotels for meals etc., they had picnics, taking food and drink with them and only had the evening meal in a hotel. The cost was greatly reduced and drink consumption and time away was also reduced. He did not believe in wasting Ratepayers' money.

Attempts at bribery by management also did not succeed. In the late 1920s or early 1930s Carlow Reid, the manager of the Fife Coal Company, sent for him for an interview. Being a victimised miner and unemployed, he wondered what he wanted to see him about. Maybe Reid had changed his mind about giving him a job.

He was ushered into a lovely, big, well furnished room with thick carpet on the floor. Then Reid put his proposition. He told him he could have a lovely office like the one he was in at present; hours at his choosing; wages agreed by him, if he would work for Reid, writing for him. As part of the deal he was to stop writing in the Pit papers (the newssheets) etc., etc. Bob of course told him what he could do with his job. Even though he was unemployed he would not be bribed (Bob was careful enough to have had a witness to this).

His integrity ran deep, even in his everyday social life. At our Socials, when we were allowed to sell alcohol, his table had always plenty of glasses in front of him, but he didn't drink much and gave it all away to others. Anybody would have given him anything. He was so well thought of, he could have been well off if he had taken everything that had been offered to him. Many who had been a little better off than most left their possessions to him in their Will. He never took a penny from anything they had left him. He tore up the Will if he had it in his possession or refused to accept anything from the family. Sometimes they left everything to him and cut out the family, but it made no difference, he would not take anything, telling the family to divide it between them.

His own family also experienced this generosity of his nature. His younger brother Willie died before him and left everything to Bob in his Will. He insisted on dividing everything equally amongst his sisters and himself. Willie lived in Orminson and wrote some very good working class poetry and, like his brother helped everyone. He knew so much they called him 'The Walking Encyclopaedia'. After he died they placed a seat at the end of the road where he used to walk every night with the other men so that that would remember him. Willie gave me some of his poems for the Young Pioneers. They were so good and numerous, they should have been published. The ones he gave me were taken from the Party rooms when I was in Russia and these are the only two I can remember:

> Thou infernal shade of evil
> I have lost to thee my soul
> Sacrificed my mind and body
> For a lump of muddy coal
> Immolated on thine alter
> All that life has given me
> And what have I got from thee
>
> Thou has given to the priestlings
> Of mad manners sordid cast
> Luxuries beyond my telling and
> Undreamed of in the past
> Given them their power and glory
> All their wealth their pomp and show
> While my portion is the spector
> Of a cold and hungry night
>
> Mad is the theme of it
> Cursed is the scheme of it
> Damned is the dream of it
> Hell is the pit
> There do we labour in
> Doing our neighbour in
> Sons hope of favouring
> Even our kin
> Slaving to give a few
> Fur coats and motors too
> While there's for me and you
> Years of Buroo

The Mining Experience

I have no experience of working as a miner, although my father was a miner, victimised and unemployed from 1921 to 1939 because of his political beliefs. For a greater understanding of the hardships endured by miners and their families read Bob Selkirk's account in Part Two of this book.

Everything changes. Nothing stands still. That's one thing we were taught by Bob Selkirk at the Marxist training class we attended. That is very true from the beginning of this century with many things. For example, the working hours of the miners. At one time they had to work nine hours each day and the Coalowners refused their request for a reduction in hours until the Fife miners took things into their own hands. They decided to work the eight hours then stop. They made their way to the pit bottom and waited until the nine hours were up before they were allowed up the pit. This was done on each shift, which meant the miners lost one hour of their pay each shift, but the Coalowners lost one hour of coal production from each man for three shifts every day. In the end they granted the miners an eight hour day. This soon spread throughout the coalfields and an eight hour day became the hours for every miner.

The Fife miners every year took the first Monday in June for a holiday to celebrate the winning of the eight hour day. Not every miner in the United Kingdom got the eight hour day at the same time. They only got it when they fought the Coalowners in their respective areas, so many districts in England and Wales celebrate it on a different month.

On Gala Day the Brass and Pipe Bands played round all the streets very early in the morning to waken the miners for the Gala. Buses and trains took everyone to whichever area the Gala was being held, usually a different place every year. Prominent speakers were booked to talk, followed by sports, races, concerts, entertainment by the Bands with a Band Contest, Beauty Contest etc. and the usual food and refreshments. So many pits have now closed the venue for the Gala for several years has been Edinburgh. That is part of the history of mining that should not be forgotten by future generations – the winning of the eight hour day by the Fife miners.

As Bob Selkirk used to say "Nothing stands still". A few years later the miners gained a seven hour day, then a five day week. Of course other industries followed suit to have their hours discussed with their employers. The next change that comes to mind is the organisation of the miners, for nothing could be gained without organisation. Each pit was organised into the Branch Union from District to District, then Area to Area, until one Union was formed for all of Scotland. At a much later date the Miners' Unions from Scotand, England and Wales formed themselves into the Miners Federation of Great Britain (MFGB). This was very good thinking, for now all the miners in the country could go forward with one voice for whatever their demand was to be.

In later years big changes took place. In the pits before the 1920s the first coal-cutting machine was introduced which cut into coal much quicker than the man with pick and shovel. Miners became unemployed and the promise of "A land fit for heroes to live in" for the men returning from the First World War became the nightmare of unemployed hardship and suffering.

In 1947–48 Bob had a serious illness and was in Milesmark Hospital, Dunfermline. From there he was taken to the Eastern General Hospital in Edinburgh. He had a big operation. After he recovered he had to go back for a check up, first a month or two between check ups then a year or two between, the final one, the doctor said come back in ten years time. Well, in ten years Bob went back, when the doctor saw him he asked what he was doing here, Bob said, "You said to come back in ten years". The doctor said, "I know I said that but I did not expect you to be alive in ten years." Bob lived on for a further ten years, the doctor died before Bob did.

The Political Background

The Russian Revolution had taken place in 1917. The workers' political parties were becoming more active in fighting for better conditions – the incentive being Russia. Following the 1926 General Strike workers became more militant following the lead of the Russian workers. They were beginning to realise the power they had in their hands. Militant workers were being elected to Town and County Councils and a Labour Government was elected. Labour Governments were elected in 1924 and 1929 and again in 1931. Ramsay McDonald in 1931 headed a Coalition Government with the Conservatives. The Labour leadership at that time said they did not have enough majority to run the country. The workers felt they had been let down. In the Local Authorities the workers were continuing to elect working class representatives to the Town and County Councils as opposed to the Coalowners and business people.

Strikes, lockouts, sit-ins, conferences, demonstrations, Union and Management discussions, hunger and unemployment marches all took place to secure what was required to make life a bit better than it had been. Working class children could now get grants to enable their parents to encourage them to have University education if they desired it. The working class were accepting the lead from their Trade Unions and the working class political parties to vote against Tory or any other party other than the working class parties.

At no time had conditions been so good for workers as at this stage of history. Free milk at school for   young children and meals at low cost. Large numbers going abroad for holidays and better, free medical attention. More married women were working and having a career, but not yet having equal opportunity with men. Family allowances were paid for children. Following the war years when more women were working, the extra money allowed them to buy the latest inventions of everything for their homes. They were beginning to feel they were middle class. Not all the workers were in that class. There were still the not so poor, the very poor, unemployed and the elderly.

During those years Labour Governments had been elected but were not acting up to the expectations of many of the electorate, so the biggest change of all took place. We had a Tory Government elected with a woman Prime Minister.

The younger generation – never having experienced a Tory Government – were about to find out what it was like to have Tory rule. There were great expectations of having a woman Prime Minister, but I don't think that anyone in their wildest dreams ever imagined that anyone could be as ruthless as Margaret Thatcher. She made it her job to make sure every concession won by the Trade Unions for their members over the years were taken from them. A legal stranglehold was imposed on the Trade Unions by the Government to restrict the help the Trade Unions could do fo their members.

During the miners' strike of 1984–85 more police were on the picket lines with their batons and horses than there were miners. She had a go at every section of the workers. Teachers and nurses had big demonstrations and strikes, the like of which had never been seen before. Civil Servants – at one time not allowed to join a Trade Union – now took strike action. Maggie Thatcher was never happier than when she was closing down the many pits, steelworks, shipyards, hospitals, hospital wards and schools.

Her Tory Government introduced budgets which hit the pockets of the workers with increases in VAT, gas, electricity and prescription charges. Privatisation of everything she could think of took place, including transport, water, gas, electricity, telecommunications and even prisons. As a result unemployment went up by leaps and bounds. Homelessness with thousands sleeping on the streets was at an all time high.

I never enjoyed anything on television as much as I did seeing Maggie Thatcher shedding tears as she went into her car from 10 Downing Street (I did not feel even a little sorry for her) that day she was voted out by her own gang. She wanted a classless society, she left behind a moneyed class and a moneyless class society.

The departure of Maggie Thatcher does not mean the departure of Capitalism. I hope the next election will see the end of Tory Government. Maybe those who thought that their lives had been better than their parents and grandparents and voted Tory, will see it was not the Tories their parents had to thank for their children having a better life, it was the militancy of the workers fighting Capitalism.

New houses were beng built with inside toilets and baths, the coal company houses with no running water and outside middens were being pulled down. The street lamps were being changed from gas lighting to electric and the beginnings of motor transport was taking over. These changes masked the hardship that still faced the working class. Bob Selkirk's activities, recorded in Part Two of this book and best read in his own words, involved most of the campaign issues with which we are now familiar: working conditions; housing; unemployment; police oppression; benefit claims; pensioners; the 1933 Hunger Marches and electioneering.

The emergence of Fascism in the 1930s heralded an era of opposition and activity in which Bob and the Communist Party were fully involved with Willie Gallacher. Several Cowdenbeath comrades volunteered for service in the International Brigade during the Spanish Civil War and George Jackson of Cowdenbeath lost his life in the conflict.

The opposition against Fascism escalated with the start of the Second World War and married women, as well as single women like myself, found employment in ammunition factories. Bob Selkirk's 12 years as a victimised miner also ended. He was offered a job in No. 7 Pit at Cowdenbeath and also worked on a RAF station and Rosyth Dockyard. Different trades and workers all followed suit.

After the Second World War ended bigger changes took place. Working conditions in every trade improved. Shorter hours, holidays with pay, a five day working week were some of the gains made by organised workers. Civil Servants joined their Union; new houses were being built; new improvements were taking place in the home, labour saving devices were being made such as washing machines, vacuum cleaners, electric irons, carpets for the floor, wireless sets, gramaphone and wireless sets were being made into one piece called the 'Radiogram'. Grocery shops were selling pre-packed foods so that less time was spent queuing for food that had to be weighed.

The biggest change of all was the Health Service. I recall that during my school days in the early 1900s nurses and teachers were a class of themselves. Only girls who had parents who could keep their children at school a few years over the school leaving age for extra education were given the chance to be teachers or nurses. When I worked in Leith Hospital in 1930, when I could not get another job because I had been to Russia, I was told that the nurses were 'above' me on the social scale. I was 'only' a servant so I was not to have conversations with them or the doctors. Now medication and the doctor were free and the elderly and unemployed received dentures and spectacles free. Some workers had gone so long without teeth that they could not get used to their new false teeth and could not wear them. New hospitals, clinics and health centres were built. All of these things were not handed to us on a plate. All these things were fought for by the workers.

All these changes took place during the lifetime of Bob Selkirk. Bob and the Communist Party took part in the struggles that were necessary to bring about these changes. He worked with hand and brain for the Labour Movement. He wrote many reports and papers on a range of social and political issues, some of which I have included in this book (see pages ???). He kept up a stream of correspondence in the local and national newspapers and responded to criticisms of his views and actions on behalf of workers. If for a week or two he did not have a letter in the local newspaper, people used to ask him what was wrong as they enjoyed his letters and answers to the different arguments so much. The editor of the 'Advertiser' (the local paper at the time) used to tell him the sale of the newspaper went down when he didn't have a letter in it. There were two freelance reporters who had great respect for Bob and gave him good prominence with issues he had not been able to get support for in the Town Council.

I had the privilege or working alongside him in the ranks of the Party for 48 years and as Fife Area Treasurer for three or four years. I have not worked alongside anyone comparable to him. One could truly say "We will never see the likes of him again". When we speak about him to someone, they say they wished they could have met him. I am pleased I was lucky to have had that great pleasure and can look back on all the activities I took part in alongside him.

Bob Selkirk was one of a very few of his calibre in the Working Class Movement. As historian Professor Matkovsky said, "He was a true son of the working class". Those who knew him can never forget him.

CHAPTER TWO
LEST WE FORGET

My contribution to the book includes a part dealing with the National Front. I thought it necessary to do so because Fascism is rearing its ugly head again, in spite of millions of people being killed and millions being put to death in the German gas chambers during the last war. (The War Against Fascism.)

It seems that lessons from that war have been forgotten by the ruling class and the Nazi youth are having a free hand to brainwash the youth of today just as Hitler did. It is up to us to enlighten the young ones regarding Fascism: let them know what took place wherever the Fascist army was able to take over temporarily in certain countries. Don't let them advance, drive them off the streets.

We must let the young ones know what takes place under Fascist rules before it is too late. The incidents I have written are only a few of the brutalities carried out by the Nazis. The National Front are in other countries as well as in the United Kingdom and are actually putting up candidates in the elections. It's time something was being done. The youth are looking for help and are an easy prey for the National Front.

Don't let the last war have been in vain.

Organise against them now.

Fascism means WAR.

Gabriel Peri, Communist member of the French Chamber of Deputies and Foreign Editor of Humanite, was shot by the Nazis in the early hours of Monday, December 15th 1941. He died with a song on his lips and shortly before he faced the firing squad he bequested to posterity this immortal letter:

The prison chaplain has just informed me that I am going to be shot in a few moments as a hostage. I beg of you to apply to the Cherche-

17

Midi authorities for my belongings. Perhaps some of my papers will serve my memory.

Let my friends know that I have remained faithful to the ideal I have held all my life. Let my countrymen know that I die so that France may live.

I have examined my conscience for the last time. I have no regrets. This is what I should like to tell everyone: if I had my life over again I would follow the same road.

Tonight I firmly believe that my dear Paul Vallant – Couturier – was right when he said that communism was the regeneration of the world and that it would prepare the way for the radiant dawn.

I am about to make my contribution to the coming of the radiant dawn. Without doubt it is because Marcel Cachim was my good teacher that I face death with fortitude.

ADIEU AND LONG LIVE FRANCE.
Gabriel Peri

Bread from loaves – a true tale of Nazi Berlin

Heinz stood on the pavement by the market. He had been to his Aunts hoping to get 50 pfennig for the pictures but she had no money. In one of his trouser pockets his fingers played with a piece of chalk, a nice big piece of red chalk and he thought, since Adolf came in there's never any money over for the pictures. Blast him!

The street lamps were pale and timid against the flat dampness of the tenement block except for the beer shops and the cinema at the corner where the trams went by. The street was black and the people hurrying along close to the walls were like shadows. Three brown uniformed Nazis came abreast down the pavement, their iron heeled boots ringing as they passed Heinz. They jolted an old woman into the gutter. Great holsters hung heavy on their belts. Timing himself with care, Heinz quickly spat after them. Suddenly there was a shout, "Kill the swine," and a man, a young worker, fell against a house door. Three Nazis were onto him kicking and beating him. Heinz saw a blue spark in the lamplight. A knife flashed. The man now lay in the gutter and his gasps rose to a scream. "You murdering swine," he cried. "You can kill us if you like but you will never crush us." He lay still, trembling with rage. The Nazis gave his body a couple of kicks. "Filthy Bolshevic," said one and spat in his face. Again the iron heels rang down the pavement.

The people in the street stood silent and sullen, watching the body lying in the gutter and listening to the ring of the arrogant Nazi footsteps but no one moved. Heinz was trembling with rage. "One of us," he said half aloud. "That was one of us." He felt sick with fury and his own helplessness.

Young Heinz saw his school friend Otto beside him. Otto wore the brown shirt and shorts of the Hitler Youth, which all school children are forced to join. Heinz would never wear the uniform. His mother could not afford it was the excuse he gave. "Otto, that was one of us. Did you know, one of us?" His fingers gripped the chalk in his pocket until it snapped.

Otto gave a shrug, "Yes, but its like that now. Do you remember last year man? Things were different then. Do you remember the Pioneer Camp and the bathing and the propaganda marches into the villages and the camp fire songs? Man, I can still smell that burning pinewood. They aren't afraid."

"Of course I remember, Otto, but what's the good of just remembering. Think of now, Otto. Can't we do anything?"

"Man, don't be barmy. Do you want your head broken too?"

"But the Comrades, they do things. They aren't afraid. You know Otto, we were, we are Pioneers and are Comrades too. Listen I've got some chalk, red chalk, pinched from school. Couldn't we ...?"

Otto stopped dead. There was a laugh of excitement on his face now. "Man, Heinz what? where? when? and if they get us they'll kill us you know."

"Let them, if they get us. At Hauptbenplatz, of course, the wall by the kids' sandpit, and right now. Come on." And he strode across the Essen Strasse, down into the little square with its round fountain garden by the great bronze toads and the public lavatory by the childrens' playground.

Otto in his brown "Hitler Uniform" kept a lookout on the pavement while Heinz, close under the shadow of the lavatory wall, wrote feverishly with his chalk. Once, the tread of heavy boots came by and Otto on the pavement broke lightly into the melody of Halst Weisels song. Heinz froze tightly to the wall, holding his breath until the footsteps had passed. Then he went on working. In three minutes he was back with Otto. "Done it," he whispered, "but don't look now." Suddenly with his mouth quite dry and tasting a little sick he saw in his mind the foot high letters he had drawn. "HITLER MURDERS WORKERS AND FILLS HIS OWN BELLY."

"Look out," whispered Otto, and around the corner from Augusta Strasse came a gang of young brownshirts harrying an aged, bearded Jew. A passing police patrol looked laughingly on. Heinz spat skillfully up at the street lamp. "Otto," he breathed, "tomorrow night somewhere else." They shook hands on it. "So long," said Otto out loud. "And don't forget the group evening talk on the old Prussian Army. Hail Hitler!"

Heinz ran home. That's better than the pictures he thought to himself and in his pocket he felt the tiny bit of chalk left over. In the archway leading to the tenement he stopped. It was pitch dark and there was no one about. The loud speaker belonging to the Nazi house porter was blaring out a Nazi speech – "The Communist murder groups in Germany have been smashed for good."

There was just enough chalk. Quickly he drew on the wall by the porter's door, "RED FRONT LIVES" and then sped up the smelly, crumbling staircase. I must pinch some more chalk from school tomorrow, he thought, while waiting for his mother to open the door.

Reminiscences

In the summer of 1941 I was just over 19 years old. A former member of the Anti-Fascist Youth, for whom I had led a group in the Condorset High School, I joined up with the resistance group which later became "The Museum of Mankind Network." After dismantling this network at the start of 1941 I was arrested with other Comrades in August. We were betrayed. After being held in the cellars of a hotel and then for a few days at Police Headquarters I was transferred to the prison of Cherchais Midae (sic) in a pretty bad state. That took place over the end of August and the beginning of September. One evening around 6 p.m. my cell door was opened. A German Guard, we called "Quick Quick" because that was what he was always shouting, took me out of my cell and into the corridor. Indicating the cell on the right, he said, "Camerad Herr Morgan Frau caput, du was macht comerad Frau mit done." I knew little German and for a moment my heart stopped. He opened the door of the cell. I found myself facing a man about 30 years old, lying on his bed smoking a cigarette which was against the rules. He got up and came towards me as the German shut the door of the cell. "So you're the one who is going to spend the evening with me," he said. I said I did not know what was going on. "They are going to shoot me in the morning for possession of arms – a pistol – and I am a Communist. They asked me if there was anything I wanted. I said that I would really like to pass my last evening with a Comrade."

I said to him that they took me as my cell was close to his. Sometimes there were long silences. I will never forget the agony and pain which overwhelmed me through it all. He was much calmer than I was but little by little the agony that he was going to be shot in the morning took over. We talked of everything and of nothing. He had no family, just a girl he knew. Nothing serious, he told me. Then, showing me some leaves of squared paper and a pencil on the corner of the bedstead, he said, "For my last letter. I was in a family so broken up that I had to start work at 13, at 10 if you count the work I did on the quiet. I never had the chance to play." He grabbed my hand. "I could never play, do you hear? Yet I loved to play just as any other kid does." Without really knowing why I took the paper and pencil and said to him, "If you like I will teach you to play Battleships." "What's that?" he asked. "You'll see," I said. We played for hours. As the minutes passed I began to forget and perhaps he did as well. When there was almost no paper left his eyes began to close. Footsteps sounded. "They are coming to take you back to your cell," he said. We stood up as they opened the door and he shook my hand. I embraced him. I will remember his last words, "We will see them off, these shits of Fascists." I nodded in agreement and he added, "As to their Europe, they can stick it up their arse." I was led back to my cell. I did not sleep that night. When they came to get him in the morning, he shouted to me, "Au revoir, Comrade. Long live liberty, long live the Communist Party!" I never knew his name, yet he was my friend and my comrade. His last night has haunted me for more than forty years.

Molly

Molly Kinnuman was twelve years old and had been going to school for seven years. She liked it at school, enjoyed her lessons and made many friends. One Wednesday morning lessons were interrupted by the warning. As she lined up with the other children to go to the shelter, the bomb, that maimed her, was released.

This bomb smashed her arm and both her legs. It killed forty seven of her playmates and five of her teachers. It destroyed her school.

Over the German radio the following evening the pilot of the Nazi bomber said, "All our bombs were dropped where they were supposed to drop. It was a special treat for us to be able to make a low-level attack on London in daylight. All our men will remember this treat for a long time to come. Every one of us reached the target assigned to him."

This bombing was no accident, "the sort of thing that happens in war." Such murders have happened too many times, in too many countries, on too large a scale to be accidents. Murder, plunder and torture terror are all part of the deliberate Nazi plan to exterminate and paralyse opposition to their aim to conquer the world.

"The plane which bombed the London school was one of six out of twenty four bomb-carrying FW190's and Me.109's which crossed the south-east coast and penetrated the capital. Its pilot ignored gasworks, road intersections, railway stations and other military objectives until a three-storeyed building loomed before him. He lifted his plane to clear it, and then, with a deliberate aim, dropped his bomb dead in the middle of the target he had been looking for." Daily Mirror, 21 January 1943

It was only by an arm being seen sticking up through the debris of Sandhurst Road School, Lewisham, that Molly was found. When her rescuer had uncovered her body from the wreckage she was in very great pain but asked that her playmates be helped out first.

City of Roses

Molde was known to Norwegians as the City of Roses. It was a little town lying peacefully by the shores of Romsdal Fjord. Hitlerism seemed very far off.

In April 1940 Hitlerism came. It was a clear day when the City of

Roses was bombed to rubble and the ruins set on fire. The Nazis said that the town might have been used for military purposes.

Europe's Jews

The Nazis have promised to kill all Europe's Jews. In one area alone, writes The Times, six thousand Jews are being killed daily. They are not just shot, but forced to strip and stand naked in the cold to be killed so that their clothes may be sent to Germany.

In Czechoslovakia it is now an offence for Jews to possess ration cards. They have long been forbidden to buy unrationed food.

French Resistance

"A few weeks ago the German military authorities in Paris announced that all Frenchmen under arrest for any reason would be regarded as hostages. At least five would be shot whenever a German is killed in France. The latest penalty is 50 hostages for every day until the culprit is captured." The Times, 27 October 1941

"More than 30,000 patriots have been shot or guillotined. More than 200,000 are languishing in prisons and camps where they are dying of hunger. Others, every day, are being hideously tortured. Patriots have had their limbs mangled in presses (the historical "boot" brought from the museums of the inquisition) and their feet have remained permanently deformed. At Lyons needles were thrust under the nails of victims. These men are your brothers." Statement issued by the French People's Aid, published in France, May 22nd, 1943

German Policy

"Re treatment of enemy civilians and Russian prisoners of war in Army Territory behind the battle zone. The wide range of operations in the East, the treacherous and peculiar character of the Bolshevist adversary demand the application from the very outset of extensive and effective measures aimed at the subjugation of the conquered territory. It has been learned that the requisite sternness is not everywhere being applied.

The Commander-in-Chief of the Army has therefore directed that the following principles be once more set forth quite plainly: any tolerance or leniency would be extremely dangerous, any tolerance or show of humanity towards prisoners of war will be severely punished. For your personal glory you must kill one hundred Russians precisely. This is the truest proportion: one German equals one hundred Russians. You have no heart, no nerves. They are not required in war. Exterminate mercy and compassion within you, kill every Russian, every Soviet person. Do not hold back if before you is an old man or a woman, a girl or a boy..." The official statement of the German Army High Command.

A letter to the Editor of Krasnaya Zvezda

On 17th January 1942 R. Belotserkovskaaya, the wife of a Red Army soldier wrote to the Editor of the 'Krasnaya Zvezda.'

"From the beginning of the 'Fatherland War' my husband has been in the ranks of the Red Army. Whether he is alive now or not I don't know. If he isn't let his warrior comrades know what the fascist beasts did to me, a Soviet woman.

On 29 November 1941, I and two of my children were placed in Kerch prison. I was pregnant. I was going to give birth any day and already was not able to walk. The German soldiers breaking into my flat saw this. However, they didn't bother. With kicks they shoved me into the passage and threw me on to a cart where they then slung my two children. Within half an hour I found myself in a damp cell, where there were already about thirty people, men women and children.

Here in prison I bore a child. When a neighbour in the cell began to offer me help, the German guard began to shout, "Stop or I will shoot." On the ninth day I was ordered to undress to my underclothes, take the children and go into the yard. To the question, "Where are you taking me?" the German soldier replied with a kick in the stomach. Together with me a few other women with children were sent into the yard. They were also undressed and stood in the snow in bare feet. They shoved us with rifle butts into a lorry and drove us out of town where already a large pit had been opened up.

When we were all lined up near the pit my nerves gave way. I hugged the children and turning towards the German soldiers cried, "Shoot rascals. It will soon be the end of you." At that moment shots were fired. A bullet hit me on the left shoulder blade and went through my neck. I fell into the pit. On top of me fell two dead women. I lost consciousness. After a while I regained consciousness and saw next to me my dead children. My grief was so great that once again my strength left me. It was only late in the evening I recovered my senses. After warmly kissing my children and freeing my legs from under the corpses of the women I began to crawl to a neighbouring village. Bloodstains were left in the snow. Almost every ten metres I rested.

I am still not thirty years old but now, after all the horrors of the German occupation, I look like an old woman. The Germans slew my three children, a German bullet left a mark on my body. My dear husband, dear warrior comrades, will take vengeance on the Fascists. They will be destroyed to the last man."

Grazhdnskaya Street

Grazhdanskaya Street was indeed a street of death. No living person occupied any of the windowless houses. From end to end it was deserted.

We searched in vain for a resident to tell us something of the murdered Rumyantsev family but no one could be found in the whole street.

Hitler's Nazi butchers had done their foul work only too well.
Ilya Ehrenburg, Moscow. Monday, 8 March 1943

Rzhev

Fedot Tikhomirov, the deacon of the Old Believers' Pokrovsk Church in Rzhev, is a venerable bearded man in his sixties. In Tsarist Russia Old Believers, a dissenting sect which had broken away from the Russian Orthodox Church, were bitterly persecuted.

Fedot Tikhomirov told us of the newer persecution – the desecration of the church by the Germans, the shooting of the aged priest and the herding of 137 people inside its walls without food and water for two days.

The first assault of the Nazi "saviours of Europe" against Pokrovsk Church took the form of robbery open and unabashed. Icons and religious pictures, ornaments and vestments were stolen. This done, the crusaders turned the church into a workshop for making barbed wire. The deacon said that when they implored the Germans not to defile their church and begged permission to pray there they were cursed and told to clear out of the way.

Continuing his story, the old deacon said, "On September 12 last when the Germans set fire to one of our churches on the opposite bank of the Volga, the priest of Pokrovsk Church, fetched his field-glasses and walked towards the river bank to see what was actually taking place. It was broad daylight – the middle of the afternoon. The Germans couldn't mistake the priest's clerical robes but they shouted "Guerilla" and one of them, raising his rifle, shot the priest dead. With the priest's wife I rushed to the spot but they refused to let us take away the body."

"In Rzhev I saw scenes which eclipse the most dreadful crimes ever committed on earth. Before their flight the Germans, pursuing their plan of mass extermination of the people, started a real massacre. No single person residing in Vorovskya Street escaped with his life. In one flat, in house number 49, lived the Sadov family consisting of eight members. Sadov's mutilated body lay at the threshold. His wife's skull was kicked into a bloody pulp – the villains had pounded it for a long time with the heels of their boots. Valentin Sadov, a boy of 16, and his sister Zoya, aged 15, were shot with automatic rifles. The 12 year old girl Raissa was stabbed with a knife. The remaining children were also cruelly put to death including Sadov's 18 year old daughter who was raped, then strangled. I prostrated myself and long prayed to God to punish these most hardened criminals of all times and all nations. These children of Satan did not spare the Orthodox clergy or the churches either. The priest Andrei Popov was shot by the Germans at the entrance of the church and the Germans blew up ten churches before they retreated from Rzhev. The 200 remaining residents of the town, including Deacon Feodor Tikhiriv, were forced into the Old Believers' Church of Intercession of the Holy Virgin." Metropolitan Nikolai, Deputy Patriarch of the Russian Orthodox Church, 26 March 1943

John Gibbons at Rzhev

News Chronicle 9th March 1943

Everything that is now being done on so terrible a scale was done first against Germans by Germans inside Germany. The world stood by, watched and did nothing. The Nazis learned that if they fought their enemies one by one, they had a good chance of conquering them one by one. They started the plan in Germany, first against the Jews, then the Communists, then the Labour Party, then Trade Unionists, Catholics and Protestants, one by one. People in other countries were shocked but took no action. They did not understand the consequences of allowing the Nazi plan to succeed.

The atrocities the Nazis carry out today take place, not in the heat of battle, but in cold blood. They are part of a deliberate Nazi plan. The crimes are premeditated.

The first large-scale experiments were tried out by Hitler's partner in crime, Mussolini. "For Fascism the growth of empire is an essential manifestation of virility," he said. In 1935 he sent bombers, tanks, flame-throwers and poison gas against warriors whose courage was armed with little more than spears. British medical men went to help the Abyssinians. The Government would not assist. At the British Red Cross Unit at Alomata, these doctors were treating up to 100 gas cases a day. On 4 March 1936 the Fascist planes came, swooped to low level and unloaded their bombs.

Lidice

It is nearly 50 years since the last war, the war against Fascism and today we see Fascism raising its ugly head once more. I think it would be a crime if I did not take this opportunity while writing this book of letting the younger generation of today know just what Fascism means to humanity.

We in this country were lucky in as much as we did not have German Fascists over-running this country as they did for a time in Russia, Poland, Czechoslovakia and France. One village whose inhabitants suffered at the hands of the Nazis was Lidice in Czechoslovakia.

One night in June 1942 when everyone had gone to bed, the Nazis awakened everyone and ordered all the men over 15 years to line up together. The women and children, who were told to bring all their money and valuables with them, were taken to the school and kept there till 6.30 the next morning. The men were taken to a cellar for the night. Nobody was told what all this was about. In the morning the women were separated from their children. Girls of 15 and over were sent to the concentration camps with the women. Babies less than 1 year old were sent to German children's homes or given to German families for adoption. All others under 15 years were transported to "Godiz" where the Nazis took 9 children and sent them for adoption by German families. The rest were sent for "sonderbehandlung" (special treatment) in the gas chamber. Records show that 89 of the 105 Lidice children were killed. All the men and boys over 15 years were shot without a trial of any kind. (The women who came out alive from the concentration camps did not know what had happened to the men and children till 1945.) All this because the Nazis alleged that the village had sheltered the parachutists who had shot down Reinhard Heydrich, the chief of the Nazi Secret Police Forces in the occupied territories.

The accusation against the Lidice people was a lie. The Germans had no proof whatever that they had even known about the murder of Heydrich. The razing to the ground of Lidice was part of the brutality of the German Fascist. The parish priest, Josef Stemberka, was offered a chance of mercy if he would renounce his congregation. He replied, "I have lived with my flock for 35 years. I shall die with them." He was shot with them. Not a male inhabitant remained alive. They were thrown into a common grave. The houses were blown up and burnt. Every building was demolished. This was a lesson to all the Czechs – this is what would happen to anyone who tried to do anything against the Nazis.

After the war the world's workers helped the Czechoslovakian people to build a new Lidice Village and the old one was filled with roses paid for by the world's workers.

Lidice was chosen as a symbol to show the might and invincibility of Fascism. After razing Lidice, the Nazis put a fence round the devastated site and posted placards at intervals reading, "Whoever approaches this fence and does not stop on order will be shot."

Visitors visiting the Lidice Museum saw the last photos of the people and their homes before the tragedy. There were also documents to show the terror – photos of the murdered men and of Nazi soldiers desecrating the cemetery. They saw the miniature glass coffins containing the clothes the miners had left at the pit. At the head of the little coffins stood the miners' lamps. It was this strong every day life that the Nazis wanted destroyed: miners at work, little children at school, women returning from their work in the fields. The Nazis photographed their own crimes. They had motion pictures and snapshots of the bodies of the men lying in rows with SS men standing by.

The Nazis thought that the name Lidice would be forgotten but they were wrong. All over the world different countries either built a village and called it "Lidice" or re-named a village "Lidice". Women in villages so poor that their children had to go without shoes on their feet sent a message to the women of Lidice, "Women of far away Lidice, widows in concentration camps, who do not know where your children are, our home is your home. We shall always think of you."

What could be as cruel as taking these children away from their mothers and mothers from children for all these years, not knowing what had become of each other. Nazis are cruel. Its their purpose in life to be cruel. Every one must do as they want them to do or suffer. We must not let them get to the younger generation of today and fill their heads with their ideas as was done by Hitler and the National Front. Learn from the lessons of the last war and get organised against them now before it is too late. Capitalism breeds Fascism. Fascism breeds war.

Tanya

Tanya was a Russian girl at High School, who wanted to leave school to join in the fight against the Nazis behind enemy lines. Her mother was not keen on her leaving school and naturally was afraid she would get killed fighting the Germans. Without telling her mother Tanya left school and joined the guerilla fighters.

She was very good and brave behind enemy lines but one day she was captured by the Germans. They hated the guerilla fighters and they tortured her most terribly because she would not tell them what they wanted to know. It was the middle of winter and very cold when they ordered every one in the village to line up on either side of the street.

They made Tanya take off her clothes. Then they cut off all her hair and made her walk through the snow the length of the village between all the villagers. She had to do this several times before they tied her from a tree and hanged her. Soldiers guarded with guns ready to shoot anyone who tried to help her. They would not let anyone take her body to give her a decent burial. The guerilla fighters eventually got her and buried her. This was done to Tanya as an example of what the Nazis would do to the villagers if they did anything against the Germans.

These are a few examples of what took place during the war against Fascism. Are we going to let this happen again? Don't let them brainwash the youth of this generation before we do something to stop them. Get organised now in every working class organisation to destroy Fascism before it destroys us.

The Soviet Union

Bob Selkirk was so pleased about the Soviet Union, the first workers republic in the world. In 1917 when the Revolution took place it was a backward and immature country, an agrarian country with no big industries. The majority of the population could neither read nor write.

In such a short time it had accomplished so much in spite of the fact that the whole capitalist world was against it. With the help of the international working class the Soviet Union had been transformed to an industrial and agrarian country. Industrially they had overtaken Britain and their aims now were to overtake America. This was before the war against fascism took place.

Schools and universities were built and every child was advised to go to the university. Doctors and nurses are in attendance at places of work. In the summer holidays cildren could go to holiday camps. Pioneer Palaces were built for the children to spend time in after school hours. Transport, at a low fare, has never increased – 3 kopecks for the trams from one end of Moscow to the other. A lovely metro was built which is so clean and beautiful it has to be seen to be believed. To go all round Moscow on the metro is only 5 kopecks. The first man and woman in space were from the Soviet Union.

After the war the Soviet Union was faced with the tremendous task of regaining all that the people had achieved before the Nazi invasion.

The Soviet Union had lost 20 million lives as well as the destruction of large parts of their country. The 'cold war period' had started because the capitalist world were hoping that the Soviet Union would not recover so no help from them was forthcoming.

In a very short time the Soviet Union had everything well in hand and cities were rebuilt. To achieve this, big sacrifices had to be made by the people. During the war years life changed, as we ourselves know, but more so fo the people of the Soviet Union. They had Nazi soldiers on all fronts. When I visited the Soviet Union in 1975, one of the girl translators in Leningrad told us that her mother was a school girl during the war. One day the Germans bombed a warehouse where sugar was stored. It caught fire and the sugar ran down the street. When it cooled, everyone was scratching for the sugar in the road. They were so hungry they ate the dirt along with the sugar.

It was no easy task for the workers of the Soviet Union to transform their country from feudalism to socialism. Foreign banks would not give them any assistance. Sacrifices had to be made by the workers. Members of the Communist Party gave 50 roubles of their wages every month to the Government. On their free day they worked, where it was needed most, without pay. Lenin worked alongside the workers on his free day.

Because the Soviet Union was no longer under a system where man was being exploited by man, it was able to plan the economy. The socialist system is based on a planned economy. First, on Lenin's advice, came the electrification of the Soviet Union. In 1928 the first 5 year plan was started. It was completed in less than 5 years. Five year plans were continued one after another until 1941 when fascist Germany invaded the Soviet Union.

At that time one could say that the Soviet people were realising what it was like living in a socialist economy as against an economy where man is exploited by man as in capitalism. The Soviet Union had made great advances. Electrification had been accomplished, the Driepar Dam and the Metro in Moscow were built. New houses and more hotels were also built. Soviet scientists and medical achievements became known all over the world. The Red Army took on 75 per cent of the German army and drove them right out of the Soviet Union.

Leningrad, Stalingrad, Odessa, Kiev, Sevastopol and many villages had all been invaded by the Nazi Germans. The Nazi invaders destroyed and burned 1,410 Soviet cities and towns, over 70,000 villages, 32,000 industrial enterprises, 100,000 collective and state farms. Material damage sustained by the Soviet Union was 2,569,000 roubles, one third of the country's national wealth.

During and after the war years the young generation must have had a different outlook on life than their parents and grandparents. The older generations had at least enjoyed a little of the results of a socialist system. All the younger generation had to look back on was the hardship of trying to stay alive, hunting for food and fighting the Nazis.

The government restarted their 5 year plans. It was very difficult to know what to do first. So many things needed to be done. With no help from the outside world and some of the best organisers in the different phases of the economy killed in the war it was understandable that mistakes were made in planning the economy.

The red flag will fly again stronger than ever. I was told by a Soviet Union visitor that Soviet Union workers had money in the bank for commodities they could not buy and there were commodities in warehouses that the people did not want. This must have been as a result of bad planning on production and market sales. The younger generation did not know what the older generation had suffered in order to build a socialist society. I think they thought the grass was greener on the other side.

It was also true that after the war some people who were in privileged positions used their positions to benefit themselves and their families. This was not accepted in the earlier period and was dealt with immediately it was known. What we don't know is how much of what happened in the Soviet Union was helped by capitalist provocateurs who do a lot of damage.

These are some of my thoughts of what might have been the reasons for the collapse of the Soviet Union. But I am sure the Soviet Union I knew will live again even better than before.

As I write this the Soviet people are seeing vast changes in their Health Service. In the 1960s 6.3 per cent of the annual budget was spent on Health Care Service. After the collapse of the Soviet Union only about 1.7 per cent is promised but sometimes even that is not given. Hospital care is still free but services have fallen sharply and hospitals cannot give the help needed. A few private western-style hospitals have opened and one in Moscow last spring was charging £617.28 annual fee for membership, £37.03 per visit and £123.45 for ambulance service. The average wage of the workers is £80.24 monthly and sometimes no wages. These facts are from the 1993 International Federation Red Cross Annual Report on Russian health.

Those who visit the hospitals are mostly drug addicts, alcoholics and helpless elderly people. Those problems did not exist 5 years ago. I feel so sorry that those Russians, who sacrificed so much over the years to bring about the Russia I knew, are suffering so much today. The USSR will live again.

> *If you dam up the River of Progress*
> *At your peril and cost it will be.*
> *That river will sea-ward despite you*
> *'T will break down your dams and be free.*

CHAPTER THREE
RETIREMENT

At the age of 80 years Bob retired from the Council, but the ratepayers of Cowdenbeath would not let him retire, they continued to go to his home to ask for his help. One such case was a woman who was looking after a mentally disabled boy who was unable to do anything for himself.

He had to be washed, fed, carried about everywhere, looked after night and day. She had a washing on the back green everyday. This woman gave her whole life looking after the boy and all she wanted was a little extra money to replace some articles the boy required.

Her Councillor in Lumphinnans had been refused when he had applied for her, so she came to see Bob. In his opinion he thought she had a good case. Bob was also refused on her behalf but he did not let it rest there. He wrote to every committee he knew and people on the different medical organisations, as well as M.P.s. He fought her case for more than one and a half years, when finally one day she came to tell him he had won her the extra money. That was the kind of person Bob was. If there was the slightest chance of winning anyone's case he never let go till the bitter end, no matter how long it took him.

Many ratepayers came to Bob for advice, but before they told him their problem, they would say they had not voted for him but came to him because they knew he was the best one to help them and they knew it would be private. Bob assured them he was Councillor for all Cowdenbeath ratepayers, whether they voted for him or not anything spoken between them was private and would remain that way.

On the early morning of the 9th August 1974 Bob Selkirk died after a short illness,in Milesmark Hospital, Dunfermline. Bob had died at 5.00am in the morning and the Radio Station broadcast his death with the news.

I had an appointment at the X-ray Department that morning at 9.00am. I awakened at 5.00am and the first thing I thought of was when I am in Dunfermline I will go and visit Bob before I came home. I got out of the X-ray Department too soon and knew I had better go home first for I would not get to visit Bob until the doctors had made their rounds. On arriving home my mother told me that Jean, Bob's youngest daughter had been round to tell me Bob had died at 5.00am.

Bob was only 3 weeks in the hospital before he died and during that time had lots of visitors. At visiting hours there were often more than eight at his bed every night and the nurses just let them stay. Three or four weeks before Bob died he said to me, "Mary, you know I am on the way out". I told him he was going to live to 90 (he was already 86). I thought when he's 90 I'll tell him he's going to live to be 100 years. I wanted to keep him from thinking about death

One night later when I went round to read the "Morning Star" to him (he had lost the sight of one eye) he said, "Mary, I can't remember the words of the Red Flag and the Jim Connolly "Rebel Song". I repeated them to him, then he asked me to sing them.

Bob died on the Friday and was cremated on the Monday in Dunfermline. The Co-op shops put the announcement in their shop windows. Every department manager was at the Crematorium as well as the General Manager, Board members and some staff. All the Miners Clubs in and around Cowdenbeath had a bus or buses booked for their members. Buses were booked by workers at the Rosyth Dockyard who clocked off their work at dinner time to get to the Crematorium. Old age pensioners also made their way there.

The funeral parlour at Cowdenbeath could not let every one in. After the service they all walked behind the hearse through Cowdenbeath High Street to the Miners Institute where they then boarded buses. There were people on the High Street all the way up and the staff that were on duty in the Town House all were outside standing at the gates till Bob went past.

There were people standing either side of the street at Crossgates and an odd one or two all the way in to Dunfermline. The Crematorium could not hold everyone in spite of everyone being crushed against one another, as well as every space being stood in. John Gollan, General

Secretary of the C.P.G.B. took the service at Cowdenbeath Funeral Parlour and Alex Maxwell the Communist Councillor took the service at Dunfermline. The Red Flag and the International were played and D. Campbell sang the International, but everyone was so overcome with grief they were unable to join in. We had all lost such a dear friend.

People of all political opinions were at the Crematorium. The Minister of the Cairns Church, Rev. McLeod, was one who also sent flowers to Bob when he was in hospital. Bob was recognised as being such an honest and outstanding fighter for his class.

Sorrow and sympathy from Moscow

Moscow,
August 1974.

Dear Mary,

A real shock to me was your letter. I cannot describe my profound sorrow to know the sad news about Bob – such a brilliant, wise and strong man, a true Communist.

Please pass my sympathy to Bob's family and friends, and his Party mates. Bob's friends in the Soviet Union shall remember him for ever.

Dear Mary, please accept my gratitude for you kind words as well as my best wishes.

Warmest congratulations at the 57 anniversary of the Great October Socialist Revolution.

Affectionately,
GALLINA

Funeral Oration
Spoken by Councillor Alex Maxwell

Members of the family, comrades and friends, on the 9th day of August at 5.00 o'clock in the morning, Cowdenbeath lost its greatest citizen, and we a comrade whom we loved and honoured.

Bob Selkirk died as he lived – fighting to the end, but this was one fight even he could not win, for Death must come to all, to whom life has come.

In Bob's case it was a life spent in the struggle for social justice, and few men have devoted their time and energy so totally and completely in service to their fellow men.

Our loss is immeasurable, and we mourn his going. To his wife, to Bob, Chick, David, Chrissie and Jean, we extend our deepest sympathy in their hour of sorrow. They know that all of us share their sense of personal loss.

Bob was born on 29th May, 1887 in a miner's row in Armiston, the eldest of a family of six.

In that miners house with its stone floor and damp walls, began a life spanning 87 years, of tremendous change, and of personal involvement in all the great struggles of the Scottish working class in the 20th Century.

It would be impossible for me to do justice to the history of his 87 years. But in his own words, "....it was a history of strikes, demonstrations, marches, evictions and wars". The great miners strikes of 1921 and 1926, the two world wars, the Spanish Civil war, the misery and the unemployment of the Thirties, the hunger marches, the election contests, the continuous fight for social justice for the working people.

In these events, Bob played a historic role, in the days of Gallacher, the Moffats, Maxton, McLean, Bob Smith, Jimmy Hope, Davie Proudfoot, McArthur, Alex Campbell, and a host of other Scottish and Fife leaders of the workers.

He has done us a service by placing his history on permanent record, in his autobiography the "LIFE OF A WORKER" written at the age of 80.

Each of us gathered here today will have his own memory of Bob, and he touched our lives. There were few people who met him who would not be affected by his manner, his thought and his activity.

For all his outward calmness, for me a characterisation of the poet John Donne best described him. "All his life, he was a man of Fire."

He was fired with conviction, determination and optimism which inspired all of those whom he honoured by calling us comrade.

He devoted his life to the working class, at tremendous personal sacrifice to himself, and his family, to build a society, based not on private profit but on co-operation for the common good. His vision and confidence of the future was expressed in the final words of his book, when he quoted Burns, "Its come yet for a' that, That man tae man the world o're, Shall brothers be, for a' that."

His early brutal days in the pits, under the coal owners in Fife and the Lothians and his travels to Australia, and the bestiality of the first world war, convinced him of the evil and corruption of Capitalist Society. He described it as legalised robbery, the lawful exploitation of man, by man. He was largely self-taught, and from his early days, he was an avid reader, studying the works of the early socialists, thinkers, economists and philosophers.

It was a natural development that he should become a founder member of the Communist Party, and he remained so, all his days.

All his energies were consumed in the fight for a new Socialist Society.

He was an outstanding Communist, he was a teacher, a guide and an inspiration to us all. He welcomed the emergence of the first Socialist country in the world – The Soviet Union, and all his life he was its staunchest supporter. In that country, which he visited four times, his name is held in honour. He had the outmost confidence in the working class and in the certainty of the ultimate triumph of Socialism. Even in moments of despair he would patiently reassure and inspire others with his confidence. He could explain the most complex problem in the simplest terms.

Even in his last days when I visited him to cheer him up, it would be me who would come away, re-charged and feeling 10 feet tall.

He played a leading role in many fields. His outstanding work in the Co-operative Movement, as General Secretary of the Scottish Old Age Pensioners, and Editor of their papers, and among the unemployed in the hungry Thirties.

But most of all he will be remembered for his service to his beloved Cowdenbeath. As a Town Councillor in Ward 4 for 32 years, his work as a Councillor was incomparable. There can hardly be a family in our town and many outside it, who have not sought his advice or help. No-one was turned away, irrespective of class, colour or creed. Thousands benefited from his service. Often it took him two hours to go from his home to our rooms, as person after person stopped him for advice.

He took up every case, or grievance, even the most impossible and pursued them with determination and tenacity. He despised bureaucracy and officiousness and pity the poor official who acted in a high-handed way with any citizen.

In the Council he fought vigorously for everything which would improve the quality of life for ordinary working people.

In his view nothing was too good for those who produced the wealth of our country.

He was the master of the Council Chambers, when he rose to speak there was always an air of expectancy and reverence. He was skilled in the cut and thrust of debate, executed with a pawky humour, which left his opponents speechless.

The advances made in our town over the years, whatever credit others may claim, were largely due to his vision and persistence.

I was privileged to work alongside him, and Willie Sharp, our Communist Provost, for a number of years. I was his apprentice, and he patiently trained, educated and guided. Even after he retired he kept a close watch on our actions, and many is the time I have gone to see him and been scolded for an ill-thought statement or action.

For his service to our town, he was given the highest honour, The Freedom of the Burgh, becoming the first ever Communist in Britain to do so.

But no one can fully measure how much the people of our town owe him. Despite his success as a Councillor, he was a modest man. He sought no honour or reward for himself. He could not be bought or bribed.

He lived simply, enjoying the affection of his family, his friends and comrades. He had many opponents, but few enemies.

He was affectionately known as "Auld Bob", it is true he was old in years, and possessed the infinite wisdom and understanding of a man who understood people and life. But his outlook was always young. He loved children and was never too busy to spend time with them. He had the optimism, the energy and the enthusiasm of the young.

At the age of 75 when other men have settled for what they know, he began to learn Russian, so that he could speak, read and write the Soviet language. Up till the end he received magazines and newspapers from his friends in the Soviet Union, which he could translate himself.

His greatest fear, was of the danger of nuclear war, and the ultimate destruction of mankind. As a warning he often repeated to us a statement by the late President Kennedy, "Every man, woman and child lives under a nuclear sword of Damocles, hanging by the slenderest of threads, capable of being cut at any moment by accident, miscalculation or madness". He saw this as the key issue of our time, the peaceful co-existence of countries of different social systems, an advocate of total disarmament.

And now he is gone. No more that letter in the press, the pawky wit, the advice, the help, the words of wisdom, re-assurance, the pricking of our conscience, when we slip a little.

But Death had no terrors for Bob. It may have brought regrets at the thought of leaving those he held dearest on earth. But the consciousness of a well spent life is all sufficient in the last sad hours. Lenin said;

"Man's dearest possession is life, and since it is given to him to live but once he must so live as not be seared with th shame of a cowardly and trivial past; so live as to have no torturing regrets for years without purpose; so live that dying he can say – all my life and all my strength were given to the finest cause in the world, the liberation of mankind."

Few men have more fulfilled that Ideal than Bob Selkirk.

At a moment like this, when we are mourning, he would have asked us to dry our tears and lift our heads, and to take up the cause he fought for, which is marching on, proud and triumphant all over the world.

The world is a different place, when first he began his life, in that cottage in Arniston, and this is due to people like Bob Selkirk all over the earth. There would be no regrets as to how he has spent his life.

And as we say our last farewell to our dear father, friend, comrade, teacher and inspiration, let me end with these words of the poet Robert Browning – which express my feeling at this time:

> *We that had loved him so, followed him honoured him,*
> *Lived in his mild and magnificent eye,*
> *Heard his great language, caught his clear accents,*
> *Made him our pattern to live and to die.*

Good-by Bob – Well done.

PART TWO

CHAPTER FOUR
'THE LIFE OF A WORKER'
A reprint of Bob Selkirk's Autobiography

My story cannot be a history of the past 80 years, but it is a brief outline of my recollections of strikes, demonstrations, marches, evictions, elections and wars: an outline sketched against the background of momentous changes in the period covered by my lifetime.

Childhood

I first saw the light in the year 1887, in a typical house in a miners' row in Arniston, Midlothian, being the eldest son in a family of six of whom I am the only survivor. The houses in this row had stone floors, damp walls, dry closets and middens and the drinking water had to be carried from the street well some two hundred yards away. No Public Health statistics are available for this period, but I do know that my mother, an aunt and an uncle died before they were forty and I had scarlet and typhoid fever before I was eight years of age.

Early memories

One of my earliest memories is of the 1894 miners' strike, their first national strike. I can remember very clearly roaming the countryside looking for something to eat, turnips or potatoes from the fields. This strike lasted seventeen weeks, much hardship was caused to the miners and their families, but the main topic for years afterwards was not the hardships but a statement by a spokesman for the coalowners that the coalowners were on the verge of granting the men's demands when the men's leaders called off the strike.

The turn of the century

Around the turn of the century many new and deeper pits were being sunk, the small individual coal owner was on the way out and limited companies were coming into the picture. Labour was becoming more mobile and frequent flittings were the order of the day. During my school days I can remember living in Arniston, Bonnyrigg, Halbeath, Slamannan and Newcraighall but I think this was rather exceptional even for these days when the segregation of the miners was disappearing fast.

School days were interrupted to allow me to start work down a small coal pit on the moors near the mining village of Eastfield in the Slamannan area. My job was to pull a sledge along the face to the road

The 1842 Report of the Royal Commission on Children's Employment in Mines contained this sketch of children used for dragging sledges containing coal from the coal face. Mine-owners still employed children like Bob Selkirk 57 years later to do this appalling task.

where the coal was filled into hutches. This job only lasted a day or so when my father had a row with the gaffer over payments and we flitted to Newcraighall. The School Board was stricter in this district and I had to go back to school until I was fourteen. The morning after I was fourteen I was back at the pits, picking stones from among the coal passing along moving tables. These tables were the first primitive kind, rattling, screeching metal contraptions that never seemed to halt, the din being terrific and clouds of dust continually floating around. It took a long time to get accustomed to them and many youngsters, despite harsh parental persuasion, found it impossible to carry on at this job.

The wage paid for this work was 1/3d per shift. This could not stand parents giving much pocket-money and after a few months I went down No.12 pit for 2/5d per shift. My first job was to accompany the night-shift fireman, Mr Dewar from Gilmerton, on his inspection rounds and then help him repair the timber supports for the roof. The seam was almost perpendicular and the coal came down to the roadway where it was filled into hutches through stone built spoots. The fireman crawled along the coal face and shouted down the spoot to me. If he did not shout I had to warn the oncost men and they investigated the cause of the failure to shout.

After this I had all sorts of jobs: watching fans which drove fresh air into stone mines, pony driving, hanging on hutches at foot of wheel braes, drawing hutches etc. These hutches were big, unwieldy boxes or trucks on wheels and built at an angle to suit the inclination of the workings. This heavy and sometimes brutalising work was carried out on a very monotonous diet of cold tea and bread and butter. For dinner we usually had scotch broth, boiled beef and potatoes. This nourishing diet helped to make up the energy lost in the pit, but one was very lucky if there were any ham and eggs or cakes for tea. These were rarities for miners around 1900.

A glimmer of light

It was while living in Newcraighall that I remember puzzling over the fact that nearly everyone displayed dislike for the men who argued that all this country wants in South Africa is the gold and diamond mines. These men, labelled as pro-Boers, had a very unpleasant time. I can picture clearly one small dark man surrounded by a hostile crowd at the corner opposite our house.

It was in Newcraighall that I listened for the first time to a socialist speaker. He spoke from a horse-drawn caravan and said things like: "The coalowners think more of their pit ponies than they do of the miners" and " the miners should own the pits." It was not possible for me to grasp the full significance of such statements, but they caused me to write to the Weekly News along the lines that the miners should form an international union and that a one day strike would force higher wages. Some of the old pioneers, like Whyte of Slamannan, refrained from criticising these crude notions and declared that my letters showed the younger generation beginning to see the light.

More flittings

We were about two years in Newcraighall. My father had demanded a higher shift wage, but the gaffer, old Geordie Thomson, had refused any increase and we flitted back to Kingseat. The next two or so years

*Hauling a "hutch" underground, the type of
work done by Bob when he started work as a boy.*

were spent working in the Flower Pit at Kelty. This meant walking two
miles each way every working day. The more modern and speedier
method of blasting the coal out, instead of undercutting the coal with a
pick, was the rule in the Flower Pit. Owing to the huge quantities of
explosives used for this blasting, the stoop and room method of working, the faulty nature of the strata and the very bad ventilation I often
walked the two miles home with heaving chest and throbbing head.

While in Kingseat, I did little else than read in my spare time. I did
not associate much with the young men in Kingseat as they mostly
worked in the local pit and we were outsiders to the natives. I read
cheap editions of University and Everyman's Libraries: Dickens, Scott,
London, Dumas, Defoe, Shaw etc. This stay in Kingseat ended with a
row over tonnage rates between my father and old Robbie Beith, the
manager. The flitting was dispatched to Newcraighall, but in the meantime my father had been told of better prospects in Ormiston and the
flitting was not taken off the railway waggon at Musselburgh but re-
directed to Ormiston, East Lothian.

More light

It was while in Ormiston, around 1905, that I heard John Young, the
North Canongate schoolmaster, lecture on socialism. I was carried

The severe working conditions experienced by the miners of Fife.

away by this lecture and considered I had only to repeat what Young had said to convert everyone to socialism. My enthusiasm was kept at fever heat by reading Blatchford's "Not Guilty", "Merrie England" and "Britain for the British". In 1906 I made contact with the Edinburgh branch of the Socialist Labour Party and became a reader of their organ, "The Socialist".

Some of the members of this branch - Tait, Jeffrey, Smith - walked regularly on Sundays to the villages within a radius of 12 miles of Edinburgh, holding meetings and selling literature. They were sectarian, dogmatic, anti-parliamentarian, anti-trade union but they were enthusiastic and they formed branches of the Industrial Workers of the World in Ormiston, Wallyford, Dalkeith and Musselburgh. These branches had a very short life.

At this time, in the small villages near Tranent - Winton, Newtown, Pencaitland - there was a small but vocal band of Blatchfordian socialists. Besides selling Blatchford's pamphlets, they sold many copies of "Our Noble Families" by Thomas Johnston, then Editor of "Forward" and later Secretary of State for Scotland. "Forward" often carried in black type the slogan, "Workers of the world unite. You have nothing to lose but your brains and some of you never had any." However, his books gave many their first jolt towards class consciousness. True, it

47

was only a tiny jolt because we saw nothing much wrong with the "Forward" hotch-potch of Fabianism, utopianism and opportunism.

The Prophet

Our Blatchfordian socialists would only work four days a week in the pit. They spent most of their time in their large gardens. One of them, nicknamed "The Prophet", would only work a three day week in the pit. He had great influence on the younger generation. Despite the modern tendencies militating against a four day week, the influence of the Prophet was responsible for many accidents caused by runaway hutches, roof supports collapsing, and pumps refusing to pump. Such accidents stopped a section or maybe the whole pit and the drawers enjoyed an unexpected game of football in the open air.

The Prophet was well over fifty years of age, almost six feet in height and spoke with a very noticeable pause between each word. Most miners at this time dreaded dismissal but it was told of the Prophet that when an exasperated gaffer shouted to him, "Put on you coat," he calmly and slowly asked, "An' whit will I dae wi' ma waist-coat?"

Local legend has it that the Prophet was poaching one evening when the Laird came across him and shouted, "Don't you know that this is my land?" The Prophet enquired, "An where did ye get it?" The Laird somewhat haughtily replied, "My ancestors fought for it." "Aweel," said the Prophet slowly, "we are baith aboot the same size if ye like I'll fight you for it."

The Prophet never denied the charge when accused of being the person who said, "If all the miners had been like me they would have been selling coals by the ounce in the chemist shop." When he was undercutting the coal he often could be heard accompanying each blow of the pick with, "One, two, three, four for the Company; one, two for the laird; one for poor Prophet." He had worked out the law of surplus value in his own fashion.

In the days when mining villages had no bus service, no wireless and no film shows, the unorthodox views of the Prophet and his like moulded public opinion in no small measure. The younger miners rebelled against going to the pithead a couple of hours or so before starting time as the old miners did. The traditional pictures of Gladstone and Spurgeon came off the walls of the miners' houses and I pinned an outspoken attack on the morals of royalty, which had been printed in the "Socialist", to the flag flying at half-mast on the Parish Hall to mark the death of King Edward.

Victimisation

The older miners had a real dread of victimisation. I remember one old miner who had been victimised simply because he stood against the local coalowner in the elections for the Parish Council. This miner ultimately took a job as a gaffer and became notorious for his attacks on the men. He tried to justify this vicious line by blaming the men for not taking action to prevent his victimisation.

The normal outlook of the managements was clearly expressed by a remark made by the manager of the Meadow Pit to a deputation. The spokesman had said, "The drawers are completely exhausted after drawing that long road and the company should shorten it." Mr McIvor, in turning down the request, said, "That's a lot of nonsense about you being exhausted. I see ye all walking about the roads at night."

About this time, 1907-8, a telegram had come into the hands of the militants. It was a message from our union agent, Robbie Brown, a Lib-Lab type, to the manager of Prestonlink Pit telling him not to start Arthur Quinn (who had been victimised in Lanarkshire) as he was an agitator. This was so much at variance with the purpose of the union - protecting agitators - that a campaign was launched by the militants against Brown throughout Mid and East Lothian. Brown did not admit his mistake but enlisted the aid of Bob Smillie and other trade union leaders. They addressed crowded meetings in all the big centres, such as Tranent, Wallyford, Dalkeith, Newcraighall and they made "realistic, whitewashing" speeches. Brown toured all the branches and won their support for the "sane line of not wanting trouble". I will never forget the rowdy branch meeting in Ormiston when Brown was being restrained forcibly by the chairman from carrying out his threat " to guzzle that young b......"

Russell, the militant justiceman at Wallyford, was one of the leaders in this campaign to protect agitators. It had always been the practice for mineworkers to take home for firewood any little bits of trees which had been sawed off to make the prop the proper length for the height of the coal seams. Russell had followed the usual custom but was summoned to the Sheriff's Court in Edinburgh and convicted of stealing timber and as a result removed quite legally from his position as justiceman. A justiceman was a miner paid by the other miners to see that the coal company did not cheat the miners out of the correct weight for the coal they filled. The company had no love for a militant justiceman and as the coal companies circulated a black-list of dismissed militants to all their pits in their district, Russell had to flit from the Lothians.

A similar legal pretext (impending production) was operated to shift Rollo, the justiceman at Smeaton Colliery. I escaped at this time, possibly because I was not so prominent and had just then met with an accident which laid me up for several months in Edinburgh Infirmary. My turn came, when the Ormiston Coal Company introduced riddles into the Meadow Pit to prevent small coal being sent to the surface. The company did not want small coal as most of their output was sold as household coal. Riddling the coal meant a lot of extra work and the company refused to pay anything extra. The men came out on strike and the riddle was withdrawn but the section in which I worked was stopped and I was on the black-list in the pre-dole year of 1909.

Still floundering

I made my way to Lassodie in Fife and was a fully-fledged brusher for more than a year. Then, actuated by the hazy desire to get away from workers who submitted to rotten conditions and the crazy notion that one could escape capitalism, I left for Australia, in 1911. The fare was £16 and the ship was German owned. We boarded the ship at Rotterdam, then came back to Southampton and stopped for a day or so in Naples, Genoa, Tangier, Port Said, Colombo, Freemantle, Adelaide and Melbourne. We left the ship at Sydney ....almost a World Tour for £16. We slept in beds erected in holds next to the engines and as it was summer when we passed through the Red Sea these conditions produced a temperature similar to that of a deep coal mine. There were one hundred steerage passengers in each hold. There were several holds and the passengers did not give any signs that they had been reared in a convent.

No escape from capitalism

I started work in the mines on the south coast of New South Wales. Late in 1912 I was drawn into a free speech fight in Wollongong. Sydney socialists had come to town to have a meeting which the police tried to stop and for a small part in the fight, I was sentenced to one month in jail. The police kept up a policy of pinpricks, and, sometimes, I met them more than half-way. It was considered best to leave for New Zealand in company with a comrade from North Wales. After a tramp through the North Island, we arrived in Wellington when the waterside strike was on. When this struggle finished, we started to explore the South Island, eventually landing in the coal township of Dennistoun. Here I had my first experience of life in a boarding house with over 50 boarders. It seemed as if everyone of them had very fixed opinions of Marx, Spencer, Henry George, Darwin and Christ. Endless discussion, away into the small hours of the morning, marked by a fanatical zeal in the defence of a point of view. It was a proletarian college.

To cut a long story short, I landed back in England in the early part of 1914 and when war broke out I was working in Choppington Colliery in Northumberland. The managing director of this colliery, Colonel Jobling, made a handsome donation to the Prince of Wales Relief Fund, but a few days afterwards posted notices at the pithead saying that in future the miners would not receive their usual rent allowance. The men came out on strike and hunger drove many of the strikers to join the army and fight to further the interests of the Colonel Joblings of Britain.

Back to Fife

I also stood in the queue outside a recruiting office in Newcastle. It was a long queue and before my turn came I went to look for grub and continued my tramp until I arrived in Cowdenbeath. I got a job in No. 1 pit, Lumphinnans, and largely under the influence of Laurence Stori-one, an enthusastic French anarchist, a few militants started a branch of the Anarchist Communist League.

We sold "Mutual Aid" by Kropotkin; "The Ego and his Own" by Stirner; "Two Pages from Roman History" by De Leon and our main slogan was "Trade Unions are bulwarks of capitalism and all trade union leaders are fakirs." We thus sowed defeatism and pessimism instead of strengthening the organisations of the workers. Actually most of the members of this branch became successful businessmen, accountants, dance band leaders, insurance agents etc. They had lost faith in the workers. They had read, not only the above, but Strickland's "Extermination of Mankind" and similar books by German authors.

The bookshop

In 1916 twelve militant workers subscribed £24 to start a bookshop in Cowdenbeath. We sold "Capital", "Ancient Society" and other Charles Kerr & Co. publications. We sold anything considered progressive even "The Strike of a Sex." We sold the anti-war literature of the time and became familiar with police warrants and police searching of our houses. Sergeant Coventry and Constable Durward really seemed to enjoy this job. On the slightest pretext, such as clothes missing from a rope or shop broken into, they obtained search warrants for our houses but they never found the literature that was sold in large quantities in Fife. We also discovered that whisky and patriotism go together and many were the threats to wreck the bookshop - usually on a Saturday night.

After the Russian Revolution in 1917 we distributed hundreds of manifestos calling upon the British soldiers and workers to follow the example of the Russian workers and get rid of capitalism. George Lansbury was the author of many of these manifestos and Smillie, Bevin and other moderate Labour and Trade Union leaders were supporting the Russian Revolution at this time. There was a great demand for revolutionary literature, for example, Sandy Niven sold enough of Lansbury's "Herald" to allow the profits to pay the rent and rates of the bookshop. The profits on the sale of other literature was ploughed back into stock.

The wide circulation of literature did a lot towards preparing the ground for the "Hands off Russia" Councils which eventually stopped the capitalist states carrying out Churchill's threat to strangle Bolshevism at its birth. Even leaders as far to the right as Willie Adamson did not oppose the "Hands off Russia" Movement.

Revolutionary ferment

This was indeed a very lively period in Fife. There is no doubt that the action of the Government in deporting Gallacher, Clark and others from Clydeside was a factor in the preparation of this ferment. This assisted in carrying the spirit of Red Clyde to other parts of the country.

The campaigns conducted by John McLean, Gallacher, Maxton, Bell, Houston, Tom Anderson and a host of others from Clydeside roused the people to anger against capitalism. Of course, this work did not begin with the deportations or the Russian Revolution but the campaigns were now reaching much larger numbers of people and more workers were listening to Marxist lectures.

After the war ended demonstrations against hunger and evictions were the order of the day. The surface workers' strike in 1919 was a magnificent struggle but it is recognised now that correct leadership had not been given to these mass struggles despite the efforts of Marxist lecturers. Widespread anger at the cowardly shooting of James Connolly, the wounded leader of the 1916 Irish uprising; intense indignation at the tactics of the Black and Tans in Ireland and a big sale of Connolly's pamphlets made it inevitable that help should be organised for the Sinn Feiners and their tactics imitated under different conditions. Help did reach Ireland - foraging parties went out to the fields to get butcher meat for the soup pots. A retired army captain came over from Ireland to drill the workers' army formed by Jack Leckie. Many wrong and foolish things were done but the masses were on the move and learning from their experiences.

Still floundering

There was much activity but we had not learned the lessons of the Paris Commune and the Russian Revolution. We had the Socialist Labour Party with its doctrinaire organ, "The Socialist"; the I.L.P. with its sentimental "New Leader"; "The Industrial Workers of the World" with its songs, the most popular of which were parodies on well-known hymns; the Anarchist Communist League with its papers and The Reform Movement with its organ "The Worker" which had Gallacher and J.R. Campbell on its editorial staff. There was "The Forward" magazines published by the Proletarian Sunday School, Socialist

Sunday School, Rationalist Press Association, Birth Control League, Health and Strength League etc. There was much ado but no revolutionary party.

Tom Anderson spared no effort to popularise the Proletarian Sunday School; Burnside of Lochgelly sold regularly 40 dozen of each issue of the "Worker"; Archibald of Glencraig did much the same for "The Socialist" and there were Burnsides and Archibalds all over the country. Speakers were being developed in the struggle. At a meeting in 1919 in the Public Park, Cowdenbeath as many as nineteen speakers were available, men like Joe Westwood who was to become Secretary of State for Scotland; J. Clunie who was to become M.P. for Dunfermline Burghs; Gallacher who was to become M.P. for West Fife; J. McDougall; Heeps; Lamb; Hope and others.

The coalowners way of life

In 1920 I had written a letter to the Glasgow Evening Times showing how the workers in the Glassee Section of Kirkford Pit could quite easily have pure air instead of black damp and I got the sack some weeks before the suggested improvement materialised. I secured jobs at one or two pits but the head office ban prevented me from actually starting. I was slowly shedding anarchistic ideas but the ban meant that I had to leave West Fife and I flitted to East Lothian. I joined the Tranent branch of the Communist Party and worried the coalowners with a steady stream of letters, now under a nom de plume, to the Edinburgh Evening News. I lost ground owing to a serious illness. When I recovered, my troubles started as the management had learnt some of the nom de plumes were mine. I was sacked several times between 1922 and 1924 but not always for the authorship of the letters. The Union delegate always got me re-started until the manager on the last occasion offered to re-start me with a contractor who had blacklegged in the 1921 strike. When the strike ended, the Union had agreed there would be no discrimination against loyal workers and when I refused the job with the blackleg the Union delegate could not assist me. I had frequently cycled to Fife during the time I was in Pencaitland and so I, naturally, flitted back to Cowdenbeath.

Post-war strikes

The post-war strikes displayed new features which indicated fundamental changes in the outlook of the miners. These changes were the result of the experiences in the first World War, the effects of the Russian Revolution and the brutal attitude of the coalowners. In 1920 there was a sixteen weeks' strike in Bowhill. The strike committee raised a lot of money by far flung activities and appeals and it struck on the novel idea of issuing paper money. This took the form of promise to pay notes which the shopkeepers and traders accepted as certain to be redeemed after the strike ended. The strike committee had members who, obviously, had studied the happenings in Russia.

In the 1912 miners' strike the union permitted the coal companies to fill their usual orders, at much higher prices, from the bings at the pithead but in the 1921 miners' strike the union took the decision to withdraw all the safety men from the pits. Where the safety men refused to withdraw much persuasion was brought to bear upon them and most of the mines were flooded and big falls blocked the underground roadways. The socialists took this chance to prove that without labour the pits were only holes in the ground in spite of the capital invested in sinking them.

The Government and the companies tried to keep the pits going and there were many clashes with the police even though the pits were guarded by the soldiers. After one clash and baton charge in Cowdenbeath the strikers retaliated by breaking nearly all the shop windows in the High Street and helping themselves to the necessities stocked in the shop windows. Several Cowdenbeath miners, fighters like William Easton, Mick Moran and others, received long prison sentences following this trouble. These sentences had the effect of stiffening the attitude of the miners to the blacklegs.

The policy of the right wing leaders of the Union, as the great struggle drew to its close, aroused the disgust of the miners. Events showed that their moderate policy was defeatism and after the strike their policy was one of bolder moderation. This was demonstrated by the right wingers Adamson and Co. endeavouring to placate the coalowners by refusing to allow the use of the financial vote as provided for in the Union constitution and by using the police to try to intimidate militant delegates at the E.C. meetings. The financial vote was a democratic measure to give the branches votes in strict proportion to paying membership but this did not suit Adamson or the coalowners.

In this explosive situation the Lumphinnans branch of the Union convened a conference of all the Fife branches at which the fateful decision was taken to form the Reform Union. Philip Hodge and William Kirker, who had been chairman of the Fife Miners' Union at the age of 23, were appointed as full-time officials. Under militant leadership the Reform Union stiffened and led the resistance of the miners to the brutal attacks of the arrogant coalowners. The coalowners regarded the miners as a defeated and demoralised army but this assumption was destroyed by Reform Union activities and this was reflected in the pages of "The Miner", a paper published by the Reform Union. Selling at a half-penny it had a large sale. It was also read by the miners who refused to leave the old union and it helped to eliminate the division in the ranks of the Fife miners.

The Communist Party

The political splinter organisation decided to join the Party. William Docherty and Peter Venters were the delegates to this conference. Peter Venters acted as secretary of Cowdenbeath District Trades Council and as secretary of the Cowdenbeath branch of the N.U.M. until he died in 1958. Willie Docherty did not give up selling the Daily Worker until the same year.

The party took a firm grip in the Kirkcaldy and Methil area but in 1922 Bob Stewart had the job of re-organising the Cowdenbeath area branch and among those who attended this meeting were Abe Moffat, Alec Campbell and Robert Smith. Again, in 1924, Comrade Joss had the task of re-organising the Cowdenbeath branch and it has continued to function ever since, though with many ups and downs. At the meeting held by Joss I was appointed branch secretary and attended the meetings which were held every week in the house of J. Dick, the Fife organiser. John McArthur, James Hope and David Proudfoot were the most regular attenders and they directed the work in the area covered by the Fife District Committee.

It has been correctly said of the Fife Party in this period that our members were weak in theory and were militant miners instead of conscious Communists. As a matter of fact I have a recollection of Comrade Joss, who was taking an educational class, asking us, "What are the basic Leninist principles upon which the party is built?" No one in that class could answer. We had forgotten what Lenin had said about the organised, class-conscious leading detachment and democratic centralism and contact with the masses. We would not have been so easily stumped if Comrade Joss had asked us what Adamson had said on a particular occasion. Still, continuous attention was paid to the vital question of healing the split in the Fife miners' ranks and the young Fife party, which was, even at this time, an integral part of the Fife movement. Quite a lot was done to draw lessons from British struggles, from the Russian Revolution and from colonial struggles by meetings and by sales of the Party organ and literature.

The main task in 1924 was that of organising mass pressure on the first Labour Government to carry out a working class policy. The workers expected great things from this Labour Government but hopes were dashed by the collaborationist policy of Ramsay Macdonald and his colleagues. The reactionaries were encouraged by the grave weaknesses of the Labour Government and the workers were disgruntled but the fight in defence of wages and working conditions intensified. The mood of the workers forced the Tory Government in 1925 to give a subsidy to the coalowners to avoid a reduction in miners' wages. The Government needed time to prepare for a trial of strength with the organised workers and so conceded a subsidy.

The Fife Communists, like militants everywhere, worked untiringly to get across to the working class the significance of Baldwin's statement, "The wages of all workers must come down." Our weekly paper dealt with this in every issue and explained the class content of Churchill's frantic efforts to build the "Organisation for the Maintenance of Supplies" - as an organisation of reactionary elements whose object was strike-breaking.

During 1925 and the first half of 1926 the Fife Communists, like militant workers throughout the country, held many meetings and organised many discussion circles. Every local comrade was pressed into taking backcourt meetings and the issues were raised in the factories, at the Labour Exchanges, in the Trade Unions, Trade Councils, in the Co-operative movement and everywhere possible. The keen struggles in Fife had developed many local speakers. James Hope, Bob Lamb, J. McArthur, Abe Moffat, Alec Moffat, P.Venters, W.O'Neill, James Stewart, Bruce Wallace, John O'Neill, Bert True, W.Crooks, Andrew Jarvie, Tom Smith, Alec Campbell, J.Watt, J.Gourdie, D.Proudfoot, Jimmie Lee (father of Jennie Lee, M.P.), Joe Westwood, Philip Hodge, J.Bird, W.Kirker and many others stepped on the soap box. The workers listened eagerly to our message. They understood that their wages and future were in danger. They understood how the cry of foreign competition was being used to foster an international starvation competition between workers in order to enrich the exploiters.

Unemployment

Before leaving the Lothians in 1924 I had been promised a house in Cowdenbeath. When my flitting arrived at the railway station I called on my prospective landlord only to be told that he had decided not to give me the house. My wife and three children had also arrived and we only got a roof over our heads that night when Annie Storione, who lived in an overcrowded house in Lumphinnans Rows, gave us one of her two rooms.

I got a job in Newton Pit, Lochgelly and worked there on coal cutting machines, drawing to the stone men and on oncost work, shifting my job according to the degree of guilt the gaffer attached to my "crimes".

The Newton Pit closed down in March 1925. Other pits had closed in the post-war period and there were many unemployed men struggling for jobs. So, for the first time, I had to sign on at the Labour Exchange. The problem, then, was one of existing on less than half the near starvation wage one had got accustomed to exist on. The scale was fifteen shillings a week for an adult applicant, nine shillings for a wife and two shillings for each child. This was the income hundreds of families in every area affected by unemployment had to maintain life. Children suffered in health, more and more families crowded into rooms and old houses to save rent money, people queued for stale buns, fried bread instead of buttering it and a pot of soup had to serve for days on end. All the methods of cheap living were tried while the fruitless search for a job went on. Household furnishings faded but could not be replaced and medical men drew attention to the lowered standards of health and well-being.

In 1925, with the very active support of the Reform Union, we formed a strong branch of the National Unemployed Workers' Committee Movement. The chairman was Hugh Muirhead, who at one time had played the same role as Osborne of Wales, in acting as stooge for the employers in an attack on the Trade Union political levy. The treasurer was Alec Bryson of the Salvation Army. I was secretary and the committee was composed of Catholics, Orangemen, and Freemasons. The Cowdenbeath branch of the N.U.W.C.M. took the initiative in forming Fife branches. Soon a Fife District Council was set up and I was appointed Fife organiser.

The General Strike

May 1st, 1926 will never be forgotten. On that day the General Strike was declared. This was the most inspiring example of working class solidarity in the long history of the British workers' never ending battle for improved conditions. To the militants of my day and generation the General Strike ushered in a new era. The workers were united and in action against those who wanted to save their profit-making system at the expense of the toilers.

Miners, railwaymen, engineers, transport workers, building trade workers and clerks etc. were united in action against the unscrupulous exploiters. The Trades Councils or Strike Committees or Councils of Action were the dominating factor in many localities. They controlled road transport in many parts of Fife as in other parts of the country. They organised the pickets, the soup kitchens and the raising of money. Communists, I.L.P.ers, members of the Labour Party and the rank and file of religious organisations were engaged in an united struggle for a common objective - the defence of living standards which were already too low.

Of course, unity did not mean there were not differences of opinion on day to day tactics. There were rights and lefts. For example, at one meeting of the Cowdenbeath Trades Council the subject under discus-

sion was police attacks on pickets. I put the case for the pickets carrying pick shafts arguing that the police would not attack strong pickets if
they knew the pickets were armed with pick shafts. This was too much
for the chairman who rushed from the platform towards me shouting,
"I'll shove a pick shaft down your throat if ye try to tell me that pickets
armed with pick shafts are peaceful pickets." Feeling ran high but the
ranks were solid in a tense situation and it was based on a common
determination to win the strike.

As is well-known from tales told by elderly people and books dealing with the General Strike, the government and the right wing leaders
of the strike were astounded at the widespread solidarity displayed and
the right wingers were afraid of the consequences of leading the fight
which had been joined. This resulted in them grovelling to the Tory
Government and calling off the strike on the ninth day.

The miners fight on

Despite the betrayal, the miners continued the fight and the strike
continued for seven months, the miners fighting tenaciously for their
slogan ... "Not a penny off the pay, not a minute on the day."

In Fife, the pickets were effective in preventing blacklegging for
most of the strike; concert parties travelled all over the country and to
Ireland raising money for the soup kitchens; the public campaign of the
miners never lacked local speakers and A.J. Cook, the General Secretary of the British miners, drew audiences numbering thousands in
places like Cowdenbeath Public Park.

The betrayal of the General Strike had made the authorities bolder
and acting under their orders the police soon had a steady stream of
pickets and demonstrators arrested and sentenced to jail. Police batons
were often used. The brutality of the capitalists only made the miners
more determined and it became more difficult to prevent the adoption
of terrorist tactics. Many a time, breath-taking scorched earth proposals
were made in the basement of Lochgelly Institute and other meeting
places, but these inopportune proposals were always defeated. Near the
end of the strike some Glencraig miners, incensed by police terror and
acting without the knowledge of the Council of Action, sent the cages
down the pit rattling and uncontrolled and wrecking the shaft. The men,

arrested for this after the strike finished, were given savage sentences. Charles Mitchell and Peter Aird, members of the Communist Party which had opposed such acts, received long terms.

In Fife, the miners publicly demonstrated their hatred of the defeatist propaganda of the right wing leaders which ultimately caused a return to work. The Communist Party had led marches of as many as ten thousand miners and their wives. One of these marches was to the Union offices in Dunfermline and another to the Dunfermline poor-house asking for accommodation and food for the womenfolk and children. There was no police interference on these marches and every marcher had a big stick and a bottle of water to help them on their long march from all the surrounding places in West Fife to Dunfermline. In 1925 the government had thought to behead the working class movement of resistance by imprisoning twelve members of the Communist Party National E.C. but the role of the Communist Party in the area had been so much to the liking of the strikers that the workers flocked into the Communist Party. In some places the Party educational classes were like public meetings and we had crowded branch meetings. This meant that when the strike ended there were very little signs of defeatism in the ranks of the miners.

After the strike

In 1927 there were Party branches in most of the bigger places and pit groups in some of the pits. It was decided that a full-time organiser was required and I was appointed to this position. It must go on record that we received the maximum help from the Central and Scottish Committees in the organising of the Fife Party work at this decisive stage in our history.

The Fife District Committee had a machine able to influence the course of events in Fife. Eight pit papers were being published, each of them with a circulation of from twenty to forty dozen. The titles of these papers had a real proletarian ring. The Spark, The Flame and The Lamp showed the instinctive desire to illuminate the way ahead. The Panbolt, The Mash, The Bomb, The Red Guard and The Double Unit indicated the desire for direct action and for class sympathy for the defence of the Soviet Union Republic.

The TORCH

No. 1. ORGAN OF MILITANT SECTION : FRANCES WORKERS. 18/10/30. PRICE 1d

SUPPORT THE TORCH : IT IS YOUR PAPER.

Mineworkers of the Frances Colliery, this is the first issue of the TORCH. The purpose of the TORCH is to give full publicity to all grievances and complaints regarding wages and working conditions at the colliery, and to give a lead to the workers on all these issues. We make no claim to having journalistic or literary ability, but hope to express ourselves in clear everyday working class language, without regard to those, whose pet ideas we may run up against, or whose 'corns' we may tred on.

We want the workers of the Colliery to make the TORCH their paper by letting us know of their grievances, complaints etc. re wages, working conditions, if safety regulations are being carried out, if there is any attempt by the Colliery officials, fireman or contrators to bully or abuse the workers. All information for publication should be sent to the publisher or handed to any Dysart committeeman of the D. M. S. branch who will arrange for its publication.

RALLY TO THE TORCH!!! MAKE IT A REAL LIVE FIGHTING ORGAN!!!

:-:-:-:-:-:-:-:-0-:-:-:-:-:-:-:-:

READ & WRITE TO THE DAILY WORKER, THE FIGHTING DAILY OF THE WORKERS!!!

:-:-:-:-:-:-:-:-0-:-:-:-:-:-:-:-:

Many a night shift was worked to produce the pit papers for sale on pay day. Clumsy brushers consulting the dictionary and the Party Organ and typing with one finger became expert journalists with no fear of the law of libel. Groups of women, too many to name, and unemployed men tramped to the pits in all sorts of weather to sell the pit papers. Others, like Bobby Ronald, toured the pubs and sometimes met aggressive, tipsy contractors who felt insulted at some of the personal criticism made of them by the pit papers.

These papers reflected the revolutionary mood of the people but we were too ready to assume that the revolution was just round the corner. We threatened the local right wingers with trial by people's courts and we printed articles which described the unpleasant jobs we would give to prominent colliery managers and other reactionaries. Still, they popularised correct ideas about nationalisation and safety first and they were effective, in many instances, in securing improved working conditions. Quite often, a marked copy of a pit paper was posted to the Government Inspector for Mines. These managers bitterly regretted that they could not sack the editors and sellers but they were already unemployed.

The pit papers helped to maintain the morale of the miners at a time when the coalowners were using every trick they knew to destroy militancy. They used victimisation, intimidation, evictions and refusal to start men in the pits nearest to their village. In spite of the tactics of the coalowners the men showed real spirit in their support of strike collections, Workers' International Relief Funds, eviction fights, hunger marches and in putting forward militant candidates for elections.

Jimmie Stewart

It would take another book at least to describe the sort of worker who led these mass activities but some mention must be made of Jimmie Stewart, the leader of the left wing bloc on the Lochgelly Town Council in 1927. He was one of the militant miners who went on one of the earliest undercover delegations from this country to Russia after the 1917 revolution; he led the masses of Lochgelly when they captured the local institute during the splendid feast which had been provided for the bigwigs on the official opening of the institute; he was among the first

Communist councillors in Fife and usually topped the poll; he participated in the immense number of meetings held at the pits in the days of the Reform Union and U.M.S. and he was on all the mass pickets during strikes.

When he was a bailie in Lochgelly two men were up in front of him for fighting with each other. Sentence was, "Admonished and I would like to tell you that the people you should be fighting are the capitalists." These sentences horrified the Tories, exasperated the right wingers but were mighty popular with most people. The tendency towards by-passing the local courts that had working class magistrates became much more pronounced and cases were sent to the Sheriff's Court.

The internal Party discussions on the class and ethical aspects of these sentences were many and keen. It was brought home to us that responsibility in new spheres created problems which had no ready-made solutions but had to be solved in the light of revolutionary principles and British conditions.

The left wing bloc on Lochgelly Town Council introduced direct labour methods in the building of houses and this proved a big success. They laid the basis for a progressive policy in every aspect of council work. Unemployment, victimisation, offers of free passages to Canada and other colonies played havoc with this left wing bloc but Stewart remained a councillor for most of the time and a fighter all the time until his premature death.

United ranks

The 1926 strike experience laid the basis for the amalgamation of the Reform Union and the old union. One result of this amalgamation was the return of many of our men as branch delegates and when the elections for the E.C. of the Scottish Miners' Union came round all the Fife miners had a vote and we decided to contest every seat. The Communist Party made no secret of its desire to see fighters returned in the ballot. We issued Party leaflets asking for support for particular militants and we used the slogans: "Vote for the Communist Nominees" and "Vote for the Communist International." Adamson and Co. made the very most of a circular, issued to party branches, giving, rather crudely, the decisions of our party on a whole host of questions to be decided at the next Fife Miners' E.C. meeting. We did not go on the defensive but issued 15,000 leaflets justifying all our decisions as being in the best interests of the men. We swept the boards in the elections, with Bird and other Communist nominees beating Smillie and Co.

The right wingers refused to accept the result of the democratic vote and they, with the blessing of the national leaders of the Miners' Federation of Great Britain, formed a breakaway union. The militants then took the decision to form the United Mineworkers of Scotland. This union, with the active support of the Party and the Young Communist League, led the struggles against the ceaseless attacks of the coalowners on the already miserable standards of the mineworkers. There can be no surer guarantee of ultimate victory over the employing class than the fact that the leaders of these struggles became the popular leaders of the Scottish Division of the N.U.M. and at the same time were well-known Communists.

Mass Y.C.L.

The role of the Y.C.L. in the fight for trade union unity, which had a special character in Fife because of the existence of two rival miners' unions in the fight for proletarian discipline, confirmed the truth of the words of Kalinin, "What is particularly characterisitic of young people is their tremendous inner urge to realise their ideals in practice." This was also true of the Y.C.L. role in the unsuccessful campaign to capture West Fife and Dunfermline Burghs in the 1929 General Election. Our candidates were Gallacher for West Fife and Leckie for Dunfermline Burghs and the Y.C.L.ers showed how to campaign.

The Fife Y.C.L. had a mass membership and support which made possible a Football League which competed for, among other things, a cup presented by Saklatvala, the Communist M.P. The Fife Y.C.L. also organised successful physical culture clubs in most big centres and ran popular boxing tournaments.

The Y.C.L. organisers over this period were Alec Moffat, Alec Massie, Jack Flanagan and Douglas Wilson. I can well remember the prolonged visits of William Rust and Walter Tapsel and the demonstrations arranged for them by the Y.C.L. I chaired the first campaign of meetings for Alec Massie in this area and watched his development into a most able speaker. He took ever so seriously the building of the Y.C.L. and the correcting of the Fife Party mistakes in dictating to the Y.C.L. and the Pioneers. Douglas Wilson, in one campaign, proposed as retaliation for the eviction of miners the eviction of the General Manager of the Fife Coal Co. from his mansion. I supported this proposal but the Fife District Committee did not and the General Manager was not evicted!

The Young Pioneers

The Young Pioneers, under the leadership of Mary Docherty and guided in the early stages by Alice Brady, played a big part in the organising of school strikes for the demands: "May First a school holiday"; "Working class history in schools"; "Abolition of the strap" and "Free meals and clothing for necessitous school children."

They had a distinctive dress, a grey jersey and red neckcloth, which they wore on demonstrations; at meetings where they presented sketches such as " The Meaning of Strikes" and "Living Newspapers"; when they were selling their duplicated School Paper and when taking collections for the purpose of sending children's delegations to Russia.

At one stage some of the Pioneers decided to wear their dress to school and this gave rise to much discussion with the teachers and the other pupils. Jennie Lee, then a teacher, now a Cabinet Minister, did not

The Young Poineers were modelled on the USSR example pictured here in Moscow.

66

like their dress or their demands. On one occasion she persuaded the Director of Education to demand an apology from the leader of the Pioneers because of statements made concerning excessive use of the strap in Jennie Lee's school but the reaction to this did not please Jennie Lee or the Director.

The first maxim of the Pioneers was, "A Pioneer is the child of a worker whose first duty is to fight for the cause of the working class." It seemed apt in those times and group recitation of the maxim was very good to hear. Some of the children spoke at meetings and gave reports when returning from Russia. They sang with great gusto one of Tom Anderson's songs which was sung to the tune of Sing a song of sixpence. One typical verse said of the upper class:

Get a pail and drown them
Or a little can.
They have been a nuisance
Since the world began.

Another verse said:

All these fairy stories
Which they tell to you
Are for little children
Away beyond the blue.

They were as vocal as the Y.C.L. when marching with them through the streets singing the Y.C.L. songs or "You'll get pie in the sky when you die."

They were successful in making May First a school holiday in this area and helped to return a left wing bloc of ten candidates to the Fife Education Authority in 1928.

The Communist candidates in this bloc had in the forefront of their election programme such demands as: "No Bible teaching in schools"; "Abolition of the strap"; "School children's committees". As one of the candidates I beat Bailie Blamey who even then was regarded as a "moderate" socialist and educational expert. The people were supporting the Communist Party and this was shown in striking victories in elections for School Management Committees, Village Institutes and Parish Councils.

One of the left wing bloc was John Sneddon who later was to become notorious as the man who led the fight for a Labour candidate to oppose Gallacher in West Fife. J.Clunie, M.P.and Pat Connolly, as well as John Bird, were active members of the bloc. The last two were outstanding, when on the Education Authority, as consistent fighters for a progressive educational policy.

The Sixth World Congress

In 1928 I was elected as the Fife delegate to the Sixth World Congress of the Communist International held in Moscow. Once in Moscow who could fail to be inspired by the knowledge that this was the capital of the land where workers and peasants, led by the Bolsheviks, had carried through a revolution successfully, had fulfilled the dreams of the pioneer socialists and had thrown the exploiters from their seats of power by applying the principles of scientific socialism. One was quickly and forcibly struck by the fact that the Russian workers carried themselves differently from the workers in capitalist countries. As the British Trade Union Congress delegation reported after their visit in 1924, the Russian workers were imbued with the knowledge that Russian workers and peasants are the ruling class.

Bob Selkirk made many visits to the USSR as a delegate and was full of praise for the improvements he observed in the conditions for workers

At the sessions of the World Congress we heard statements from Stalin and other Russian leaders who had been the architects of this revolutionary change. These leaders had spent long years in prison and exile under the deadly tyrannical rule of the Czar and his minions and had been tested in the grim conditions of the class struggle waged against brutal ruling-class terror. We listened to outstanding Communist leaders from the capitalist and colonial countries and discussed these statements in our daily delegation meetings.

We heard these leaders explain the general crisis of capitalism, the partial stabilisation of capitalism secured at the expense of the masses, the significance and meaning of the colonial struggles, the danger of fascism and war, the vital importance of the unity of the world's toilers and the birth and preservation of the first socialist state.

In Moscow, where we even met school children who knew the different trends of the labour movement in the various capitalist countries and who understood the reasons for the superiority and inevitability of socialism, it was much easier to appreciate the truth of Marxist theories and what their application meant to the millions of people suffering from mass unemployment and low wages in capitalist and colonial countries constantly threatened by the horrors of war. It was easier to see in proper perspective the tasks of Communists outside Russia.

The discussions gave opportunists and sectarians the opportunity to get to know the correct Bolshevik line; it brought out the immense importance of a daily press for Communist Parties and it emphasised that it was the duty of Communists to oppose fearlessly every ideological tendency and institution, political, social or economic which militated against the development of a dynamic class consciousness among the masses whom the Communists served.

The deliberations, resolutions and reports of the Sixth World Congress, based upon a masterly analysis of the world situation, corrected mistaken policies of Communists throughout the world and sustained and guided hundreds of thousands of fighters in the trying and testing times which lay ahead. It was a real, functioning International Communist Congress which helped immeasurably the Russian people and oppressed toilers everywhere.

Second Labour Government

In 1929, as already mentioned, we put forward Gallacher in West Fife and Leckie in Dunfermline Burghs as candidates in the parliamentary election. The national party slogan was "Class against Class" and we could not truthfully be accused of being to the right of that line. Our defeat in the election had a bad effect on some of our Party members, due in some measure to our over-optimistic attitude during the campaign.

The election resulted in the return of the second Labour Government with Ramsay Macdonald as Prime Minister and once again hopes were raised in the minds of the workers of substantial improvements in working class conditions. These hopes were soon dashed when the Government announced that they were going to continue with the foreign policy of the Tory Government and when they accepted the conditions laid down by the American financiers for a British loan "to help us" through the crisis. These conditions included the slashing of the meagre allowances to the unemployed and an all-round reduction in wages. The Labour Party was split from top to bottom in this attempt to perpetuate capitalism. Ramsay and a few other right wingers went openly over to the Tories and a large scale attack on the conditions of workers was started by the National Government under Ramsay's leadership.

The new Means Test Regulations now introduced were so vicious that even M.P.s, who had voted for the regulations, were astounded and exposed their ignorance of the regulations when challenged in public meetings to say what the scale would be in a particular case. The very confident Mr. Henderson Stewart, M.P. will never forget his confusion when Mrs. Stewart, a well-known Communist fighter, proved, at a public meeting, that he could not calculate the scales in simple cases although he had just finished telling his Leven constituents that he was in favour of them. Other M.P.s got the same dose and local Unemployment Assistance Officers publicly admitted that they had not realised how low the proposed scales were going to be until they started operating them. Some Labour MPs had the grace, under mass pressure, to admit that they had been wrong in throwing doubt on the forecasts of the N.U.W.M.

Inevitably, thousands and thousands of unemployed workers, left without any income and thrown on the charity of their low paid friends, massed at the pits and factories looking for jobs and the downward trend of "starvation level" wages was accelerated considerably. The salaries of Government employees and the pittance paid to the Armed Forces were reduced and not even Naval tradition and discipline could prevent the discontent in the Navy coming to a head in a mutiny at Invergordon. This well organised mutiny sent shivers up the jittery spines of the exploiters who thought that the revolution had started.

The appeal of the National Unemployed Workers Movement, led by Wal Hannington, for united action against "this Government of hunger, fascism and war" resulted in the springing up all over the country of United Front Committees which organised meetings, deputations, demonstrations and marches. In Cowdenbeath the United Front had William Watson, defeated Labour M.P. in the 1931 election, as secretary and myself as assistant secretary. The very desperate situation made us ignore the very unpleasant comments made on Watson's "defeatist" role in the General Strike as a "sane" miners' M.P. and the Communist Party's analysis of his role when he defeated Leckie in the 1929 election.

In the industrial field, the unemployed had as very vigorous allies the influential National Minority Movement which carried through decisive national conferences and national campaigns. After 1930 the Daily Worker played a most important role.

Hunger marches

One hunger march to London had taken place during the period of the second Labour Government. Soon after the passing of the hated Means Test Regulations another London march was planned and carried through. Of course, the Government had been forced before this to modify its regulations because of the size, determination and solidarity of the demonstrations in Scotland, England and Wales.

In the succeeding period marches were organised to Glasgow, Edinburgh, Dundee and Cupar. These were enthusiastically supported by the rank and file but bitterly opposed by right wing Labour and Trade Union leaders. The marchers demanded the abolition of the Means Test, higher scales and work schemes. Had these demands been granted the schools of this country would have been modernised, more council houses and more clinics would have been built and such necessary plans as the Forth Road Bridge and the widening and straightening of roads would have been carried through. An unanswerable case on financial and social grounds was presented by the marchers but the employers required a reserve army of labour to bring down wages and the right wingers did not want to embarrass the Government in a period of crisis.

These right wing leaders must bear the full historic responsibility for dampening down the militancy of the workers thus saving the employing class from having to grant the full demands of the unemployed. These right wingers propagated the line, "Do not march, do not demonstrate, do not strike, wait for the General Election and vote for us." They trotted out the hoary lie, "The communists only want to create chaos and misery in order to achieve revolution." They poured scorn on the need for united action against the Government of hunger, fascism and war and so helped the return of a Tory Government in 1935.

Despite the "tame" socialists the mass activities did force concessions in the form of higher scales of relief, work schemes in certain localities and free meals and clothing for necessitous school children. The mass actions did provide the rising generation with a better chance of growing up as healthy and intelligent citizens and a better chance of under standing the need to overthrow capitalism.

The reactionary Fife County Council did not like these mass activities. At the most hectic period we had only one Communist County Councillor, Alec Moffat, and he was most active inside as well as outside the Council in leading this mass activity. On one occasion the Fife County Council had the married men, who marched to London, arrested as wife deserters. The Dunfermline Sheriff agreed with the County Council but collections were organised and an appeal against the convictions was made in the Court of Session. This Court agreed that the men were not wife deserters but were men who had gone on a march in order to try and improve the lot of their wives and children. This was a sore blow to the Cupar Tories but it greatly heartened the men.

It was a really big job to take hundreds of men along the open road to London. It required the co-operation of thousands of people living hundreds of miles apart. Meetings were held at all Labour Exchanges to discuss the objects of the march and up to the minute reports from the columns of the Daily Worker on activities in other districts were studied. Circulars and deputations were sent to all organisations and reception committees were formed in the villages and towns through which the marchers had to pass and where they would have to eat and sleep.

The marches drew into activity hundreds of thousands of people and aroused the lively interest of millions in the urgent problems of unemployment. The books, "Unemployed Struggles 1919-1936" and "The Problem of the Distressed Areas", written by Wal Hannington about these marches will repay close study because unemployment and the prospect of mass unemployment will always be a danger while capitalism lasts.

The marches to Glasgow, Edinburgh, Dundee, Cupar and other county towns were not such gigantic efforts as the London marches but they also required exceptional activity from the "lazy unemployed" as we were described by the "lazy Tories". Each of these marches produced some very tangible benefit for the people and they certainly helped to develop class consciousness and a clearer understanding of the root cause of mass misery. They prepared the way for the great fight against bestial fascism and for the return of a Labour Government in 1945. The unknown marchers can hold their heads high. Although they got no medals they did their bit towards making the world a better place.

They set off on these marches possibly after suffering demoralising malnutrition for months or maybe years. Their boots required repairs and their clothing was scanty even in the dead of winter. They did not know where they would eat or sleep but they were conscious of the need to endure hardships cheerfully in order to force the operation of measures to solve the problems of mass unemployment. Of course it was not all a question of blistered feet, drenching rain or life in the workhouse. The mass support of the people, everywhere the marchers travelled, more than compensated for the hardships.

The hunger marches

The first Cupar march, led by our Communist County Councillor, Alec Moffat, proved to be a great success and not only from the point of view of concessions gained. It was composed in the main of men who, as a result of a thorough rationalisation drive for the shutting down of the least profitable pits, had recently become unemployed and felt very bitter against the powers that be. They wanted to give the Cupar Tories a bit of their mind. The route taken was through as many big centres as possible and the men arrived in Cupar in very good spirits. Just before entering Cupar, a meeting was held and the men were advised not to allow themselves to be provoked by the large number of police who had been mobilised, as our main aim was the interviewing of the County Council. There were quite a number of small plantations on the next three or so miles and the men equipped themselves with a stick, sometimes a young tree, to make walking easier. There was no trouble in Cupar and our deputation was heard. The deputation was greatly bucked up by the contrast between the very adaptable attitude of the Labour Councillors and that of the Communist Councillor. The Labour Councillors, when they addressed the chairman, the Earl of Elgin, always said in an indescribable tone of voice, "My Lord", and were not content with saying it once. The frequent salutation of Alec Moffat was, "Hey sir, you are not getting away with that stuff."

No one who participated in the Edinburgh march of June, 1933 will ever forget the experience. The authorities refused to provide halls for sleeping and we slept on the most Conservative street in the proud city of Edinburgh. We slept on Princes Street and had a really splendid view of the "poor inmates" of the very aristocratic clubs on the opposite side of the street. We had our breakfast and dinner the next day on Princes Street and when we left our "digs" we were simply lost in a sea of humanity. People seemed to pour from closed doors and from all directions and the hordes of police were submerged and powerless. For the first time in the history of "puir auld Scotland" we swept through the gates of Holyrood Palace and the old walls resounded to the slogans and shouts of the marchers. Some sang the old Scots song, "We're no awa tae bide awa," but we have not been back as yet and the Princes Street Tories may have forgotten their fright. The Daily Worker was the only paper to publish this news about Holyrood Palace. Our parting gesture was one of contempt. A friendly wholesaler had given us enough bananas to serve the fifteen hundred marchers. The banana skins were placed on the points of the railings running the whole length of Princes Street. A pamphlet issued after the march was entitled, "The Three Days which Shook Edinburgh" and had a large sale.

On one of the later Cupar marches, we encouraged the idea of cyclists accompanying the marchers and cycling between the various contingents from East and West Fife. We also had an old crock which performed the same service and this gave one of the daily papers the chance of a great scoop. They described the leaders of the march riding to Cupar in a Rolls Royce. One of our chaps complained afterwards about this distortion in the press and mournfully told a meeting, "We had to shove it down a hill."

On the last Cupar march in 1937 the police, who outnumbered the marchers, made a mad rush towards the flute band which had been tormenting them all day by ignoring instructions not to play outside the County Council chambers. The deputation, taking advantage of the temporary absence of guards from the doorway, rushed into the County buildings. The County Council changed their decision not to hear the deputation and the staff of the Cupar Co-operative Society, which always catered in grand style for the marchers, excelled themselves at teatime that evening.

On a march to Dundee we were met by thousands of workers at the Ferry and quite safely broke the magistrates' ban on all street demonstrations. We got into the habit of breaking this ban while in Dundee and the police did not interfere. We were so well fed and had such large meetings in the city square that some of the marchers seriously proposed that we should keep on the march. The women of Dundee had provided food on a generous scale. After a few days of good feeding and class support the marchers, who had been semi-starved for months and months, felt that they could storm the heavens and they wanted to become part of a permanent army of unemployed carrying the message of the N.U.W.M. all over the country. It would have been a torch.

These men did not only march but played their part in the early morning picketing during strikes. One morning pickets were on duty at

Brighills, a Lochgelly pit. One of the pickets was Thomas Baillie who had met with a accident in the pit and was permanently crippled. A big policeman, after some arguing and some shoving, threatened to throw wee Tammie over the bridge. Tommie, who was a five footer, looked up the the six foot policeman and said, "Ye better mind that two can play at that game." Swinging his stick he left the policeman powerless with amazement although it was only the policeman's helmet that went over the bridge.

Eviction wave

It is almost incredible but true that local historians, who lived through this period and in some cases lived on the dole, write as if there had never been unemployment and great struggles in this area. Actually, from 1921 to 1938, there were never less than fifteen hundred to thirty hundred signing on at exchanges in the Cowdenbeath District and the struggle for survival was grim indeed.

People were often in arrears with rent and eviction decrees were obtained from the Sheriff. The evictions were sometimes due to reasons other than rent arrears, landlords wanting a house for an employee or a relative or for an extension of business. The decree was soon followed by the appearance of the Sheriff 's Officer and an adequate force of police. The tenant, family and furniture were flung out on the street. A meeting was arranged with hundreds of workers coming to the scene of the eviction. Sometimes the meeting was advertised by bell and megaphone, sometimes by a flute band. After the meeting had assembled and speeches made, the furniture was put back into the house. On some occasions we held the meeting some distance from the eviction while a group was putting the furniture back unnoticed by the police surrounding the meeting. Still, no matter what our tactics, the eviction was followed by the arrest of the militants, sometimes as many as ten being picked up. At one very big eviction fight in Lochgelly the comrades arrested were Abe Moffat, W.Spence, party organiser, Alec Campbell, myself and six others. At another Alec Moffat, myself and eight others were arrested. Fortunately the authorities in this area were a bit scared and we never got the same sentences as were imposed in other parts of the country. Comrades in Wales, for example, were getting fifteen months in jail while we were getting just a month or two.

A STONY ~~UCH~~ IN PRINCES STREET

The negotiations between the leaders of the hunger marchers and Edinburgh Public Assistance officials for help towards the cost of the transport of the marchers to their home town, broke down yesterday, and the demonstrators remained in Edinburgh overnight. Our picture shows some of them occupying the pavement in Princes Street during the afternoon, but at night they found shelter in ___ in Edinburgh and Leith.

The hunger marchers slept on the pavements of Edinburgh during the hunger march of 1933. The spikes on the railings were festooned with banana skins after they enjoyed a snack.

WITH THE HUNGER MARCHERS IN EDINBURGH

After their deputation to Drumsheugh Gardens yesterday to interview the heads of Government departments, the hunger marchers went to Parliament Square, High Street, where a meal was served from the travelling kitchen.

Willie Gallagher M.P.

Lenin photographed during the Russian Revolution. Bob Selkirk made several visits to the USSR and remained loyal throughout his life.

During the troubled period I was the Fife organiser of the N.U.W.M. and was in the dock eight times from 1926 to 1935. Some of these times I was in the dock for trivial offences in connection with speeches, demonstrations, evictions and so on and except for two occasions got off with a fine. I was evicted by the Lochgelly Co-operative Society from one of their houses even though I did not owe one penny of rent. The seige lasted for many hours. The house was well barricaded, ten people were arrested and the police attacked a protest demonstration with batons. Another demonstration the next evening was not attacked. When I came out of jail the only accommodation available was in a caravan. The caravan had obviously been built for summertime and it was not summertime. This caravan was used by the local unemployed in a protest march up and down Cowdenbeath High Street. I finally got out of the caravan by taking possession of an empty house and the authorities did not prosecute me for squatting. They were beginning to see that every arrest led to a bigger membership for the N.U.W.M.

Just about this time, there was an eviction in Hill of Beath and before getting up to address the meeting, I said to brusher Sinclair who was chairing the meeting, "Go easy. I do not want to go back to jail just yet." He nodded his head in agreement but his opening words were, "Fellow workers, if we were men at all we would chase these b ... policemen for their lives." When the battle is joined the British workers cannot be intimidated.

Unknown warriors

The Fife District Council of the N.U.W.M. had branches with memberships ranging from 1,200 in Alloa to 50 in Auchtermuchty. The daily representation of unemployed claimants at Courts of Referees, Parish Offices, Small Debt Courts etc. and the organising of the eviction fights, hunger marches and so on was only made possible by the devoted services of hundreds of semi-starved men and women.

Outstanding in this respect was Mrs. Stewart of Methilhill. She was one of a group that flitted to Fife after being evicted in Stoneyburn, West Lothian for the part they played in the 1926 strikes. The menfolk of this group could not get jobs in their home area. Her husband got a job in Methilhill and she joined the local Communist Party. She built up a reputation for untiring service. She was elected as a County Councillor for her area and was never defeated but had to retire because of ill-health. Never a day passed but she was at some kind of office in connection with sick or unemployment benefit, rent arrears, pensions. compensation etc. The officials knew she could not be fobbed off and so she got satisfaction in every case where this was at all possible. Although ill, she carried on working for the British Legion, Old Age Pensioners Association and the Communist Party until her death.

I can recall Alec Bain who was blind but who had a legal training which he put at the service of the unemployed. Angus Noble and Bain never seemed to tire in drawing up summaries and explanations of the many regulations and the thousands of umpire's decisions on particular cases. Donald Campbell was the most biting critic of those who opposed the demands of the unemployed. Peter Kinnell who, if he did not get immediate satisfaction on a claimant's grievance, always threatened to draw the Parish Clerk or other official over the counter.

As Kinnell had such a big percentage of wins in the cases he handled, the District Council was often asked to withdraw him as a representative but always refused to do so. The Exchange officials often asked that some action should be taken to restrain the criticisms of Donald Campbell but Donald was too valuable an asset in the fight. On one occasion the Exchange manager at Cowdenbeath asked Donald to shift his platform away from the exchange window as his staff could not work because of Donald's loud voice. Donald in his most impressive manner said, "Mr Steel you are the manager in there. I am the manager out here and my work is doing alright." The manager asked the police for help and Donald appeared in the Burgh Police Court. The police sergeant testified that he had heard Donald's voice one hundred yards away from the Labour Exchange. When Donald came to cross examine the sergeant he reminded him of this assertion and got him to repeat it. Then Donald asked, "How did you measure this distance? With your feet?"

All this had an unsettling affect on the presiding magistrate who, when opening the case against me, said, "Are you guilty or not guilty, Selkirk? Whatever you say, I know you are guilty." This was too much for Mick Conway who was sitting in the body of the Court and who shouted, "That's not British Justice." He was brought to the bar and the Bailie sentenced him on the spot to ten days in jail.

As organiser of the unemployed, I wrote protesting against Mick being handcuffed and led up the High Street. I wrote to Chief Constable Savi and got back the very brief reply, "You are lucky. If I were in Cowdenbeath you would be in jail, too."

It was the activities of unemployed militants that defeated all the attempts to prevent the holding of meetings at the Labour Exchanges. Attempts were often made to stop these meetings but all the attempts failed. Sometimes the police were made to appear powerless in the eyes of the unemployed. For example, the police in Kirkcaldy had arrested militant speakers who were sent to jail. The next week I was the speaker at the Exchange when twenty policemen surrounded my platform and a black maria appeared on the scene. I was ordered to stop speaking but carried on and the police withdrew. Twenty new members joined the N.U.W.M. that day.

Elections and strikes

During this period the Fife miners at different pits were forced to strike against sectional wage reductions, speeding-up, the spread-over, the dirt scale etc. These strikes were organised by the U.M.S. under the leadership of Abe Moffat and were tenacious struggles. The Valleyfield strike against the operation of a harsh dirt scale (a scheme for deducting from the weight of coal in a miner's hutch more weight than that of the dirt actually in the hutch) lasted thirteen weeks. It is on record that one of the first things that Gallacher raised on the floor of the House of Commons was the issues involved in the Valleyfield strike. He was the first M.P. to raise in this way the issues involved in a local strike. His action led to the men winning the strike and resuming work. The Valleyfield strike played a big part in the return of Gallacher in 1935 and he rendered a very big service to the Valleyfield men.

Undoubtedly, militancy generated the political understanding which brought about all the victories gained by the Fife party around 1935: Gallacher's return as M.P. for West Fife, the winning of several council seats, the winning of positions in the Trade Unions and in the Co-operative Movement.

David Fairley and I were returned in 1935 to the Cowdenbeath Town Council and right away began using our new vantage point to mobilise support for the fight against capitalism by pushing the Party's municipal policy in council discussion and in reports to the electors.

When King Edward ran away with Mrs. Simpson or vice versa, we had a discussion in the Council chamber. During the discussion on the proposal to send a loyal message we referred to George "blacklegging" on his brother and moved that as he had no stamps on his insurance card he should only get the U.A.B. scale.

We white washed slogans on the roads:

George King – 15 shillings a week
King George – £15,000 a week

A debate was arranged on the question, "Should the workers support the monarchy?" My opponent Lt.Col. Mitchell, secretary of the Carnegie Trust was so impressed by the tone of the discussion that he would not let the chairman take a vote from the large audience.

We fought for work schemes, housing schemes, clinics, modern schools, playing fields, swimming pools, more meetings for ratepayers and for a junior town council. We fought against discourteous and inefficient officials inside and outside the Council. Our meetings at the Labour Exchange, the sale of the Daily Worker and the publication of a local Town Council bulletin helped considerably to win some concessions and more sympathetic consideration for the victims of a rotten social system.

The Spanish Civil War 1936

The Fife Party fought well in the cause of the Spanish toilers. By the exercise of their democratic votes the Spanish progressive elements had secured the return of a progressive government. The reactionary forces, led by Franco and assisted by Hitler and Mussolini, organised an attempt to overthrow the government by military force.

In the campaign the Fife Party immediately began to rally support for the Spanish People's Government in order to counteract the non-intervention tactics of the right wing labour leaders in every country. My young colleague, David Fairley, addressed a lot of meetings even though he was obviously suffering from the illness which was to bring

A deputation of hunger marchers at Kirkaldy Parish Office in the 1920's. They were demanding work or more money. Bob Selkirk is holding the banner on the left of the photograph.

Bob (arrowed front row right) on another hunger march to Kirkaldy Parish Office, 1930.

A group photograph of Cowdenbeath Communist Party members and families taken during a picnic at Clune, Glencraig in 1927. (Bob Selkirk is circled).

A Young Comrades Social held on the 7th November 1928 in the C.P. Hall, Cowdenbeath. Mary Docherty is on the far left and Bob Selkirk is standing next to her.

"Flitting". A frequent experience for workers' families.   Photo: Glasgow Bulletin.

The unemployed suffered from a feeling of hopelessness and humiliation in the 1920's and 30's. The N.U.W.M. organised and assisted them.

Huge banners depicting revolutionary leaders are paraded during the Pageant of Scottish History in 1939.

Bob (far right) shares the platform during a political rally.

The Lamp

Election Organ of THE WORKERS' ELECTORAL COMMITTEE.

Dunfermline District of Burghs.   Polling Day—30th May.   1929.

WORKING MEN AND WOMEN.

Fellow Workers,

We issue this paper in order to place before you certain reasons as to why you should vote for the Workers' Candidate, Jack Leckie, on May 30th, and why you should continue to support the Communist Party after the General Election.

Jack Leckie

is the Workers' Candidate in the Election. The other Candidates, without any exception, assert they do not represent any class but represent the Nation

The Nation

is composed mainly of the Capitalist Class and the Working Class. The Capitalist Class aim at securing profits. These profits are realised through forcing the Workers to labour for much less than the value of the wealth they create

Wages

under capitalism are continually tending to come downwards. International Competition is becoming keener and compelling the Capitalists to attack wages more frequently.

Since the end of the War the wages of the British Workers have been reduced over £700,000,000 and the average rate of profit has gone up.

The Workers' Candidate

in the interests of the Workers, must fight energetically against this tendency for wages to come down.

Capitalist Candidates

claim that they can serve the interests of all sections ; pursue a policy which will increase profits for the Capitalists and increase wages for the Workers—

This is Impossible.

A Political Party must either serve the Profit-Making Class or the Wage-Earning Class.

JACK LECKIE,

THE COMMUNIST PARTY CANDIDATE STANDS FOR THE INTERESTS OF THE WAGE WORKERS.   1.712 Votes   Lab Watson = 15.263.

Women and War.

The working woman to-day, wearied and heavy at heart struggling from week to week in a desperate effort to make ends meet, has little time to devote to the "affairs" of the State. Bending over the washtub, cooking for the family, scrubbing and cleaning, it is little wonder that she fails to see the menacing clouds that are gathering over her, heralding another bloody deluge.

The world to-day is an armed camp, the earth trembles under the feet of armed men, in the air and under the sea Capitalism holds her "blood-hounds" on the leash.

The last war ploughed deep furrows on the hearts of millions of working women of all lands, who gave 10,000,000 of their sons as fodder to feed the greedy mouth of the cannon.

With hearts still bleeding from the last war, the military Moloch is athirst again, demanding the husband from the wife, the son from the mother and the sweetheart from the maid. The next war will be a war of unparelleled ferocity, compared with which the last war was but the sigh of the wind on a summer evening.

THE JACK BOOT.

And it must be so, as long as Capitalism lasts. In their mad scramble for markets, raw materials, etc., there are no laws, moral or divine, that they are not prepared to violate.

One quarter of the whole world to-day groans under the brutal iron heel of Britain's military jack boot, and Capitalism is prepared to sacrifice tens of thousands of British and Colonial lives in maintaining its "prestige" in far off lands.

The Monarchy.

Wm. Watson stated at a Cowdenbeath meeting that he was not in favour of abolishing the monarchy.

The monarchy costs over £1,000,000 per year, this is sufficient to give 10,000 aged workers a pension of £2 per week.

We say:—

Away with the monarchy—
Pensions of £2 per week for
all workers over 55 years.

Watson says:—

Maintain the monarchy.—
Pensions for all Royal
persons.

It is said that Mr Watson fancies himself in knee-breeches and wants to attend the Court, and so he is defending the monarchy.

Mr Watson used to wear knee-strings and at that time he was all in favour of defending the workers against the monarchy.

The monarchy ~~~~~~ ~~

The Next War.

War is at hand.

Field Marshal Sir William Robertson accuses the United States Officials of "speaking like the Germans before 1914."

The next war will be a war of extermination. It will obliterate all distinctions of front or rear. Air bombing that can destroy whole cities, chemical warfare, poison gases, disease germs—all these are not being prepared for play.

The only salvation lies in voting for and actively supporting the Communist Party.

Some extracts from the 1929 issue of the "THE LAMP", much of which is still relevant today - 67 years later.
Watson was the Labour Candidate and Lecky was the Communist Candidate in the General Election. The comments on future war were prophetic

Whoop! Ye Workers, Whoop!

LABOUR GOVERNMENT SEEKERS TAKE NOTE.

Are the workers of Fife aware of the fact that a miniature Labour Government has been operating in their very midst over a number of years.? Cowdenbeath holds this " proud " distinction, and the workers of Beath are not happy for this precious gift as the following will go to prove.

TOWN COUNCIL.
A Solid, Hard, Labour Majority.

These defenders of the workers' rights and privileges increased the Burgh Officials' salaries (already overpaid individuals) by £50 per year. At the same time they threatened to reduce the Burgh Employees wages. Agitation only prevented them from doing so.

Do You Know?

That Watson was educated, by the financial assistance of the miners, at the Ruskin College.

That a Worker with a college education should educate other workers.

That Watson has never led a Workers demonstration against Capitalists.

That Watson has been member for Dunfermline and Secretary for West Fife Divisional Labour Party for years.

That the roads and houses in Lassodie and Hill of Beath are a disgrace.

That Watson has represented these places on the County Council for years.

That a vote for Watson may let Beaton slip in.

That you should vote for Leckie and not allow either of the Capitalist Candidates in.

That Leckie would put up a real Working-Class fight inside and outside Parliament.

Published by R. Selkirk, Victoria Hall, High St., Cowdenbeath.
Printed by David Watt & Sons, Douglas St., Dunfermline.

him to an untimely end. At one of these meetings I acted as chairman and before he started to speak I whispered to him not to antagonise the people present. But Davie was keen to win them to our side and carried away by his feelings I heard him say, "I believe that anyone who supports Franco ought to be shot."

It was always our experience in this area that the people resented any attempts made to split the ranks. For example, the Catholic Unemployed Association had a very short life in this district.

In Fife there were exceptionally large collections of money and food for the Spanish workers. One pay night a team of over fifty with handbells and wheelbarrows went round the working class rows in our ward and the response they got took our breaths away.

Several Cowdenbeath comrades, like comrades all over the country, volunteered for service in the International Brigade which went to Spain. One Cowdenbeath comrade, George Jackson, made the supreme sacrifice. The Fife workers understood that bombs on Madrid meant bombs on London and that fascism was the common enemy of all who desired to see social progress.

Always sensitive to the mood of the masses, William Watson, M.P. for Dunfermline Burghs with Communist Party support, said in the Tivoli Hall in 1936, "Let us learn a lesson from Spain. The Tories would do the same as Franco if a government tried to carry out a socialist policy."

It was during the period of the Spanish Civil War that the Fife Party, while Abe Moffat was organiser, organised the most successful Marxist lectures. One series in Lochgelly Town Hall was addressed by lecturers like Tommy Jackson, Maurice Dobb, W.Gallacher and others and drew capacity audiences. Up to and after "Munich" big teams tackled patriotic places like Dunfermline with posters and the sale of the Daily Worker.

Eve of war

The drive for large scale re-armament started by Baldwin, who had won the 1935 General Election for the Tories with the misleading cry, "Collective security and not arms is the Tory policy," meant that many of the idle millions began to find employment in places like Rosyth, Donibristle, Crombie and other government war depots. Re-armament also increased the demand for coal and the Fife Coal Company lifted the ban on the employment of militants. I and many others, banned from the mines for ten or twelve years, secured work in the pits. I started in No. 7 Pit, Cowdenbeath. I got a nice easy job to break me in and a special handshake from the manager the morning I started. I attended the first branch meeting and put up the case for higher wages for certain grades. I also proposed that every member ought to get a printed notice announcing the branch meetings and that a summary of the most important branch decisions ought to be printed and given to every worker in the pit. These were necessary steps as only a handful of members attended the meetings.

The following week I was shifted from my easy job and put on repairing and backbrushing. This was a dirty job amidst water and intense heat from an underground fire. I only lasted a few months as acute dermatitis developed on my hands and arms. I was in this pit when the Russo-Finnish war was raging and the pit bottom echoed to threats from patriots to knock your head off. Of course, we lived to see these patriots having to acknowledge that they had been easily kidded by press tales. Events proved that the Red Army, supposed to be a comic opera army during the Finnish war, was the only force capable of holding and routing the Hitler hordes. It was noticeable that the people, who had been most annoyed at being deluded with the silly stories about the Red Army, were the least liable to be carried away by the witch hunt in the years after Hitler was defeated. Those, who did not display too much annoyance at being made to appear very foolish over the Finnish war, were most easily carried away by the similar false-hoods forming the basis of the new anti-communist campaign.

Recovering from dermatitis I secured a job labouring at an Air Force station. This was my first real experience of the way in which the big Public Work contractors waste the taxpayers' money. The contracting system was based on time and materials plus profit. This system is a real school for sharp practices.

Greatly helped by Willie Gallacher and the Daily Worker, the Fife Communist Party did a great job in the exposure of Chamberlain's policy of support for Hitler as a means of waging war against the Soviet Union. Our party was, at the same time, in the forefront of the campaign for decent air raid precautions and in Fife detailed proposals for underground shelters were worked out. I and many other party members were in leading jobs in the Civil Defence. I was head warden in the Fourth Ward, Cowdenbeath and at the end of the war received a presentation from the wardens, most of them Labour Party supporters, athough they had not liked our advocacy of the second front and increased production during the long hours on duty.

A bailie

After Hitler's attack on Russia and Churchill's denunciation of Chamberlain's policy of no alliance with the Soviet Union, I was elevated to the bench. Remembering Jamie Stewart and his experience as a magistrate, I tried to persuade my Labour colleagues to cut out the rule of standing up when the magistrate enters the Court Room. I failed in this but the procedure became much less formal. The fiscal did not like this informality nor the habit of admonishing for petty offences instead of fining and fining a mere two shillings and sixpence when there had been broad hints before entering the Court Room that a fine of some pounds was expected.

I was also selected to represent Cowdenbeath on the County Council. The Red Army had done what mass pressure in the days of mass unemployment had failed to do. While on the Fife County Council there were nine Communist Councillors and the Party policy was pushed during this period. I was on the Social Welfare Committee along with Mrs.Stewart and together we fought to improve the conditions in the poorhouse at Dunfermline. The day room was like a mortuary - no papers, no games, no wireless. We had complaints that eggs were a memory. We saw attic dormitories where one man's feet were touching another man's head because the beds were placed end to end and there was no space between the beds. I was on the County Council long enough to have the experience of having an old man touch me on the shoulder and say, "We are getting eggs now." I also saw most of the bad conditions disappear.

A gaffer

While working at the Air Force station, a national appeal was made for ex-miners to return to the mines. I volunteered and was given the job of being gaffer at the coal cleaning tables at the Peeweep Pit. I had about twenty youngsters and half a dozen adults to do the very heavy work involved in cleaning wartime coal. The work was far too heavy for the young folk of 14 to 18. It was rather difficult, at that period of increased production for the war against fascism, to manoeuvre adequate rest periods for them. I was a popular gaffer with the workers but not with the management. There were five moving tables. Stones from the first table had to be thrown over the first four tables along with the stones which came from these other tables before they were loaded on to the fifth table for discharge into the redd wagons. There was a conveyor belt under the floor for these stones but, due to faulty construction, it had never conveyed any stones and the young folk had to suffer.

Some improvements were secured after the Party pit group raised the question of this conveyor which had never conveyed; the question of underground mistakes responsible for a large number of stones the youngsters had to shovel several times and other grievances hindering production. After a few months a flying splinter from a big stone which was being broken up damaged my eye and I was several weeks in Edinburgh Royal Infirmary and told not to go back to the mines.

Rosyth scandal

I then started work in Rosyth Dockyard to the great surprise of those who knew of the longstanding ban on militants at this Naval Base. The state of affairs in Rosyth was simply disgusting - a criminal waste of labour and materials which betrayed the effort against Hitler.

I recruited enough members in my shop to the Transport and General Workers' Union to form a branch and was elected branch secretary and shop steward. Thus entrenched, I began a scathing exposure of the criminal waste. I drew up statements and sent them to the Ministry of Labour, to M.P.s and to the press. Only the Daily Worker and the Dunfermline & West Fife Journal printed them.

All sorts of excuses were given for this wanton waste of materials. The wanton destruction of stores required by the lads at the front, by the child and adult victims of the Nazi air raids and by resistance fighters everywhere continued throughout the war period.

A high ranking official of the Ministry of Labour came over from Edinburgh to interview me and after I had given him the facts he said, "I believe you but it is only a few Communists who are protesting. Most of the men in the dockyard have had years of unemployment and they are afraid that they will lose their jobs if they say too much and some of them are looking for promotion." The best elements in the dockyard supported my efforts and most realised that it was only the shareholders of the big combines who gained from this waste. A firm would supply, as per regular order, linoleum, brushes, cycles, glass, dynamoes, lavatory fittings, electric light globes, blankets, paint, timber etc. These goods would be placed on the surplus stock list for disposal to a favoured merchant or were simply destroyed by being burned or buried in the sea where land was being reclaimed. The one thing, apparently, which could not be done was reducing the order supplied by contractors to the Admiralty.

This was infuriating, especially when one saw gangs of workers cutting up blankets at a time when children in the bombed towns were reported to be going without blankets. Then one saw large quantities of glass being broken up when children were shivering in rooms without windows in Coventry, Clydebank and other places. At that time many a worker expressed the opinion that it was better to risk the search and take the goods out of the gates rather than see the goods destroyed.

The Communist Party struggled hard to transform the wartime Naval Base, with its great engineering and other shops, into a factory for the manufacture of peacetime goods to supply the clamant needs of the British people. After the war, in our pamphlet, "A Plan for Fife Prosperity" we put the considered case for this switch. We managed to have quite a lot of civilian work done, enough to prove that the Naval Base could have made quite a big contribution towards repairing the ravages in Britain's economy, but the profitmaking monopolies won and the base continued to be used as a jumping off ground for the shipping of equipment required for the massacre of Greek and other workers struggling to be free from fascism and exploitation.

The Fife Party after the war
After the war finished the Fife Party carried through a lot of activities: factory gate meetings, public meetings, educational classes and

publication of pamphlet and Gallacher broadsheets. We replied to the anti-communist campaigns; we explained why the Second Front had been held up and we showed the value of international agreements like Potsdam and Yalta. Possibly, we placed too much emphasis on the co-operation of capitalism and socialism at Yalta but we did carry worth-while campaigns of explanation and made it very clear that the Labour Government returned in 1945 ought to stick to a working class policy both at home and abroad in opposition to Toryism.

Our support among the workers was still growing. In 1947 we nearly won a majority on Cowdenbeath Town Council. Similar advances were being made in other parts of Fife following Gallacher's return in the 1945 General Election although his opponent, a Labour candidate, received a large vote.

In Cowdenbeath, over confidence and the action of an expelled member, in standing as an "independent communist" in the same ward as one of our candidates, prevented us getting the majority which would have given us the chance to show that the Communist Party policy is the best under all circumstances. We would not have revolutionised life under capitalism but we would have eased the position regarding payment of rates by the old people; we would have introduced direct labour and charged lower rents than the authorities who gave large sums as profits to house building contractors; we would have had better social services such as playing fields and pools; we still would have had a Junior Town Council, an Information Bulletin, more Town's meetings and would have carried the fight to the Government and the County Council. Our own weaknesses prevented the people getting this experi-ence and developing a clearer political understanding of what hurts them.

This was our peak point. The people were forgetting how the Red Army had saved the world from fascism, the anti-communist poison was taking effect and we began to lose seats. The voters were loyal to Labour although Labour was not loyal to them. We were slow to recog-nise the factors producing the change in the mass outlook. The Cowdenbeath experience was the experience throughout Fife. We lost County Council seats and we lost seats on the Co-operative Boards but we still ran many mass campaigns during this period.

Defeat ... then victory

In 1948 I had a serious illness of which John Fernie, agent to Willie Gallacher M.P. said, "You had not one foot in the grave, you had both feet." I was in hospital for several months and the enforced curtailment of activities during a long convalesence led to my defeat by 26 votes in 1951. The local reactionaries were jubilant. They enjoyed ranting that the Communists are finished in Cowdenbeath. But in 1952 I was again returned to the Council with a majority of over 100 votes. The eleven Labour councillors were arrogant and dictatorial over the single Communist. I worked out a tactic of putting in for every Council meeting twenty questions on ratepayers' grievances but they countered by revising the Standing Orders and only permitting two written questions. I tried moving and seconding my notices of motion but the Provost ruled this out of order.

So this cat and mouse game went on until, in 1955, Willie Sharp was again returned to the council and we have held two seats until the present time. In 1962 we lost the third seat in our ward, the Fourth Ward, by 8 votes. Another 20 votes would have been cast but for the lack of cars in the evening. In 1956 the candidate who beat me in 1951 was standing for re-election to the local Store Board and I opposed him and knocked him out and we defeated him for a seat on the Council too.

The electors of the Fourth Ward or the majority of them, who had voted for Communists consistently since 1935, stood firm against all the anti-communist slanders. This is a record of consistency in election behaviour which it would be hard to beat especially when it is consistency in support of the "bomb throwing, religion destroying bolsheviks." This support was maintained and Alex Maxwell, Planning Officer, N.C.B. was returned to give the Communist Party the three seats in the Fourth Ward.

Concluding reflections

This is written in 1967, at 80 years of age, after a period during which I have held the position of Town Councillor, director of the local Co-operative Society, Communist Party Branch Secretary, General Secretary of the Scottish Old Age Pensions Association, Editor of Scottish Pensioner and secretary of the Cowdenbeath branch of the O.A.P. Association.

My many experiences in these positions, reinforced by three visits to the Soviet Union of which the most recent was in July 1967, have confirmed the political convictions which have led me to participate in the struggle for social justice. It is impossible to enumerate these experiences in detail. It is only possible to outline the lessons drawn from taking part in the efforts to establish a social system which would give humanity the full fruits of scientific and technological progress.

The capitalist world

On 12th July, 1963 the London Times said, "There is something seriously wrong with this country" and the Manchester Guardian agreed with this authoritative diagnosis of capitalist Britain. The pro-monopoly, pro-American policy of the Labour Government since this diagnosis was made has not improved the position but has made the situation worse. This is painfully obvious when one considers the growth of unemployment, the unused productive capacity. It is agreed by nearly everyone that much more money is required to raise housing conditions, schools, universities, hospitals, recreational and cultural facilities up to the standard essential for the fullest possible development of the potential of our citizens but the money is being wasted on suicidal nuclear and conventional armaments by politicians blinded by the ideology of the rat race.

One of these politicians, Sir Cyril Osborne, recently pathetically exclaimed, "Who would work for 9d?" thus proclaiming his belief that even if the country gives surtax payers several hundred pounds per week they ought not to do anything for the benefit of the community. His colleague, Mr. Enoch Powell asserts the he is never happier than when surrounded by rich men thus proclaiming his belief that profit-making even from the manufacture of napalm and nuclear bombs is the be-all and end-all of worthwhile human effort. The result of these beliefs, having a society built on the immoral principle of legalised robbery, can be seen in the mass poverty of the unemployed, the sick and pensioners and the insecurity of the higher paid workers by hand and brain.

The socialist world

Russia, a backward country under capitalism, is, after a short period of 50 years, leading the world in many spheres: the fight for total disarmament; the liberation of colonial peoples; liberation from the cruel and ruthless exploitation by imperialist monopolies; exploitation, supported by the armed forces of the capitalist class, as in the horrible war waged by the Americans in Vietnam and the negroes in the United States.

Russia, despite the devastation caused by the intervention by imperialist powers in the early days of the revolution and by two world wars, is leading the world in social security because they have public ownership of the means of wealth production and planned production for the good of the community and not for profits for a privileged parasitic minority. This example and the example of other socialist countries strengthens the efforts of progressive humanity to get rid of the ideology based on mean and despicable self interest.

The socialist world is pulsating with youthful vigour, marching forward confidently, planning and rebuilding on a tremendous scale and evolving a higher form of democracy, sparing no effort to win support for the policy of peaceful co-existence of countries with differing economic systems, the only policy which can save humanity from nuclear disaster. The peoples of the socialist world understand the truth embodied in the grave warning given by the late President Kennedy when he said, "Every man, woman and child lives under a nuclear sword of Damocles, hanging by the slenderest of threads, capable of being cut at any moment by accident, miscalculation or madness." There is no doubt that President Kennedy was in the position to know the dangers of the situation created by the insane drive for individual gain.

More and more people are striving for world peace. More and more people are propagating the truth that the anti-social system based upon the legalised exploitation of man by man must be replaced by socialism as preparation for the establishment of a social system based upon the principle of from each according to his ability, to each according to his needs.

Only thus can we secure world peace and social justice. Only thus shall the vision of Burns, the Scottish bard, be realised. The vision is embodied in the words ...

It's coming yet for a' that,
That man tae man the world o'er,
Shall brothers be for a' that.

BOB SELKIRK
Cowdenbeath
4th August, 1967

COWDENBEATH
TOWN COUNCIL ELECTION, 1946

FACING BOTH WAYS!

The Right Hon. Joseph Westwood, M.P. and Secretary of State for Scotland, has been in Cowdenbeath and, according to the local papers, he congratulated Cowdenbeath Labour majority on their remarkable record regarding housing, etc.

However, in a letter to William Gallacher, M.P., he says something very different, viz. :—"*In conclusion, let me say that I do appreciate fully the unsatisfactory situation to which attention has been drawn, and the need for the most urgent action to effect an improvement in living conditions in Cowdenbeath.*"

Actually, Mr Westwood refused to designate Cowdenbeath as a needy housing area, and the Scottish Special Association cannot build any more Weir houses here until he does so.

The Town Council ordered over 400 temporary houses in 1944, and when Mr Westwood spoke only 11 had been occupied. Words have no meaning when this is spoken about as a "great record."

The position is as bad so far as Water, Sewage, Playfields, etc., are concerned, and Mr Westwood knows that subsidence does not fully explain the rotten situation.

WHY NO INQUIRY ?

Why did he not agree to an Inquiry ? Would not this have been the best way to dish the Communists who had asked for the Inquiry ? He did not agree to an Inquiry because the Communists would have been proved right in their criticisms, and his Labour colleagues wrong.

Think it over, and if you want the Town run in an efficient way — you will vote Communist. This will not cause a revolution, but it will bring immediate improvements.

VOTE
Selkirk, Hutton, Venters, Moran,
FOR
Immediate Improvements.

Issued by W. Harkins, Election Agent, Room 8, Victoria Buildings, High Street, and Printed by Given & Paton, Cowdenbeath.

TOWN COUNCIL ELECTION, COWDENBEATH

Tuesday, 6th May, 1952 — Broad Street School

PUT COWDENBEATH IN LEAD

Bob Selkirk   Communist Councillor

MARY DOCHERTY   Fourth Ward.

W. HOEY—Third Ward.

Make One into Three Councillors

Mary Docherty and Bob Selkirk on Party work in Cowdenbeath.

At the Store Gala, July 1958, with P.Kinnell and Jean Hall.

Enjoying a picnic with comrades.

Bob (centre) on the annual "Water Drive" to the local waterworks.

PART THREE

COLLECTED WRITINGS FROM
BOB SELKIRK'S DIARIES AND NOTES

CHAPTER FIVE
THE TRUTH ABOUT THE SOVIET UNION

Capitalism versus Socialism

It is wrong to expect the upper class, which control Radio, T.V. and national press and other means of mass communication to tell the truth about the Soviet Union, the first Workers' Republic. No outdated class in history has ever given up this privileged position without using every weapon, including lies and violence to retain as long as possible a retrogressive role in society.

The Cold War

As a result of the flood of Cold War falsehoods many people have a distorted picture of things in the Soviet Union. Of course it is true that everyone in the Soviet Union works for and is paid by the community. It is also true that no citizen in the Soviet Union occupies a privileged position through exploiting the needs of fellow citizens. It is considered immoral to rob other citizens.

Social Services

"Prevention of illness" is the motto of the Health Service, and this is of a very high standard. Pensions for old age, disability and sickness are from 60 per cent to 70 per cent of wages and in some cases 100%, without any deduction from wages, the State bearing the full cost. It is certain that anyone really contrasting Capitalism with Communism must come to the conclusion that it is essential for the future happiness of mankind to take a hand in organising to establish Socialism in every country.

In Capitalist countries there are a large number of citizens who work for and are paid wages or salaries by the community, including Central and Local Government officials, University lecturers, teachers, nurses, doctors, M.P.s, the members and employees of National Boards, Trade Unions and Co-operative officials etc. It is generally accepted that many of the above mentioned categories are dedicated and feel much more secure than the employees of private companies and small businessmen.

Defending parasites

It cannot be this feature, which is common to Capitalism and Socialism, that gives birth to the illogical notions embodied in Cold War propaganda, so it must be the feature making illegal the legalised robbery of fellow citizens, to which hypocritical worshippers of the freedom of the individual are opposed. Naturally these ideological luxuries camouflage their real aims by constant repetition of idealistic platitudes, in the same way as such inevitable products of Capitalism i.e., Hitler, Mussolini, Rachman etc., but it is obvious they only want to rob legally their fellow citizens. Frequently we hear the parrot cry "We only want profits in order to invest in the up-to-date machines". A few minutes thought is sufficient for the realisation that investment by private funds cannot be geared to national requirements, except in a very haphazard and chaotic way. Only under Socialism can production and distribution be scientifically planned, so that every citizen gets the opportunity of the best possible living and cultural conditions. Monopoly capitalists want maximum profits without consideration for the well-being of the masses.

Socialism superior to Capitalism

There are many facts to prove the superiority of Socialism to Capitalism. One of the most convincing is the fact that one hundred and nine nations are living in harmony in the Soviet Union. While in the the Capitalist world we have Ulster, Indonesia, Nicaragua, Cyprus, South Africa, Rhodesia, Latin America and the Middle East etc. It is often asserted that trouble in these areas are due to the backwardness of the masses, but this is proved to be untrue by the great progress made by the formerly oppressed and down-trodden peoples in the Soviet Union.

Site for own house

In the Soviet Union any citizen desirous of acquiring his own house gets land from the State, free of charge. Of course, if the owner wishes to sell his house, he cannot sell the land, but it is transferred to the new owner free of charge. Grants and loans are at a low rate of interest and are available if required. Most of the houses are built and are rented by the State factories or the Trade Union.

CHAPTER SIX
DEBATE AT COWDENBEATH

"Should Jubilee Celebrations be supported?"

Falling on the variance of opinion shown locally in connection with the King's Jubilee, a Public Debate on the question of "Should the Jubilee Celebrations be supported" was held in the Tivoli on Wednesday evening, arousing considerable interest. The principals were Colonel Mitchell, Chairman of the Carnergie United Kingdom Trust (affirmative), and Mr Robert Selkirk, representing the Communist Party (negative). The hall was filled almost to capacity and the Chair was occupied by the Rev. R. Douglas Potter. Opening the debate Colonel Mitchell, who claimed to be outside the politics, described visits he had made to various parts of England and Scotland during and prior to the Jubilee Week. He said he was amazed to find everywhere the generous and sincere respect shown towards our King. On Monday 6th of May, he willingly accepted an invitation to speak at Cowdenbeath, but he regretted to say that the planting of the trees in the West Church grounds and at the service in the Public Park, he did not find the same anonymity.

The speaker went on to say that it was his experience that often he found sections getting separated from one another and he illustrated his point by referring to the different points of view to be gleaned from various national newspapers. He had made a point of always trying to read both sides, proceeding to illustrate his point further with chapters from his own life. He stated that as the son of a Minister he had been brought up in a very narrow life and that it was only by getting with men of different classes that he had grown to learn more of his fellow men. He was sure that the difference of opinion regarding the Jubilee Celebrations was due to a misunderstanding.

The King had stated he was entirely non-political. In the course of his reign had all kinds of Governments, except a Communist Government. From personal knowledge the speaker claimed that the King had worked with equal loyalty and straight-forwardness that each of the parties had. The King occupied a peculiar position and no one could suggest that he spoke in the interest of any one section. It was a great thing for the people to have so impartial a Sovereign. The King did not govern. He said that was a tremendous asset.

Colonel Mitchell went on to emulate the different situations that had arisen during the reign of King George. He had risked his own person during the Great War and went far forward into the trenches. In events which followed the war, it could not be said that he had favoured any one section of the people at the expense of any other section.

He attributed the failure of the Monarchy in various other countries to the partisanship shown and added that they in Britain still had an entirely democratic country. That fact was one of the greatest possible tributes that could be paid by historians to our King. The speaker went on to describe the great voluntary service performed by the King and his genuine interest in young people of the country had been show by the lead he had given in allocating his Jubilee Trust Fund for the benefit of youth.

Mr Selkirk in giving the negative view said that there had been sufficient happenings since the Jubilee Celebrations and after that allying the statement of his opponent he was sure they were correct in organising an anti- Jubilee demonstration.

He claimed that they could not keep politics out of the subject and pointed out that a leading writer in the Daily Mail had advised the Government to take advantage of the patriotic atmosphere being created by the Jubilee and have a General Election soon. Then they had the Daily Herald, the official argument of the Labour Party, who had supported participation in the celebrations appealing to the Government not to have a General Election now because it would not be playing the game. These writers, the speaker declared, knew that the Tories had developed the best in a patriotic atmosphere and he claimed that everyone who supported the Jubilee Celebrations were supporting the National Government.

Colonel Mitchell had referred to the splendid traits and characteristics of the King and of his adopting a neutral attitude. No one, he declared, could adopt a neutral attitude as far as politics were concerned. He asked if it were possible for the King to sign Part Two of the Unemployment Act, in the best interest of all his subjects.

Colonel Mitchell had also referred to the King's admirable qualities and his connections. Mr Selkirk said they could possibly get a Bookmaker who was a loyal husband, a worthy citizen and a good father to say in debate that his family should be supported. They could have the same type of individual as the Publican, speaking on behalf of drink, but would people agree that these things should be supported? Hanratty, Bottomly and Scots Jimmy have been decent individuals in a private capacity, but that was no reason why they should support highway robberies and turn our children out to be burglars.

Proceeding, Mr Selkirk said that it had also been stated by his opponent that the King, during his twenty five years reign, had done his very utmost for his subjects. Just imagine going to a worker on the Means Test, who, just because he had saved three hundred pounds was denied benefit and asking if he considered if the King, on signing that measure, was acting on the behalf of that individual.

They had to approach the subject under review, from the point of view of the working class. It might be said that he was introducing politics, but they in the Communist Party said that the King must bear the responsibility for anything that he signed. Stalin in Russia accepted responsibilities for the action of his Government. Did the institution of the Monarchy help or hinder the outstanding problems of our time? Which in the words of Lloyd George were the curse of plenty.

Concluding, Mr Selkirk asked his audience to consider the illogical results of the Jubilee and if they did so in the light that they had been presented to them, was sure they were justified in demonstrating against the celebrations.

After an opportunity had been given for questions both speakers summed up. At the request of a member of the audience, a vote was taken and resulted in a unanimous finding in favour of Mr Selkirk's point of view. This was the report from the Cowdenbeath Advertiser, following the debate at the Tivoli.

CHAPTER SEVEN
REST HOME FOR WOMEN

The Communist members of the Fife County Council were successful in having a resolution carried, asking that steps be taken to build rest homes for women having a nervous breakdown. At present such sufferers are treated at Stratheden Hospital, but this is part of Springfield Asylum and there could be no worse arrangement. The resolution also asked for increased Maternity Homes Accommodation. The Fife County has only one Home, a very small home in Newport, miles and miles from from the industrial belt of the County. Scotland is the worst of seventeen European countries for death rate among Mothers and Infants and we simply must get improved Maternity and Child Welfare Services to remove this blot on the reputation of Scotland. Raise it sharply with your Councillors.

Extracts from the 1946 (monthly) July Bulletin.
Near the end of the 1926 General Strike the fight against black-legs became a most important phase of our activities. The Press devoted much more space to tales of Miners going back to work in England and Wales. The leaders of the other Unions, in order to justify their desertion of the Miners, had to put the case against continuation of the Miners' struggle. All this had the effect on the moral of the Miners and some districts decided to return to work. In Fife the question on the agenda was "Should Fife Miners remain out on their own? A big percentage of the Miners were for the continuation of the struggle and this was reflected in the monster demonstrations held in Fife several days after the Miners in many districts had returned to work.

Like many others in Mining districts I have been twice in Dunfermline Sheriff Court, once for making a seditious speech in

Lumphinane and once for demonstrations. This marked me down as one of the dangerous persons who should not be employed. The party had become so much stronger as a result of its correct policy in relations to the Miners' struggle that we were now in a position to form a Fife District Committee and I was appointed Organiser of the Fife Party, which had active Branches in the industrial part of Fife.

The lessons of the General Strike were carried to the workers in such a manner as to maintain, despite defeat and betrayal, the militancy of the Fife workers. One remarkable feature of the long drawn out fight of the Miners had been the great solidarity of the unemployed. Not one single case of an unemployed black-legging on the Miners had come to light. This was undoubtedly due to the fact that the unemployed were organised in the National Unemployed Workers Committee Movement whose motive was "black-leg proof". The unemployed participated in all the other phases of the struggle of the Miners, in demonstrations, pickets, meetings and raising money for soup kitchens etc. I had been Fife organiser of the NUWCM, but gave this up when I became organiser of the Fife Communist Party.

The record of the Fife Communist Party is a record of which we can be proud. Fife Communists know that they have saved thousands of workers from suffering unnecessarily at the hands of the employers and bureaucratic administrators. We know from tangible results built by mass struggle in the days of the Pit Papers. We know our Daily Worker has played a vital role in preventing reactionaries from further depression of the living standards.

The fight for radical and fundamental improvements in the living and cultural conditions of the mass of the people will yet be successful and the sacrifices of the countless thousands of unknown fighters will not have been in vain. We see humanity ever striving onward, urged on by the effects of the changes and methods of production, these changes being tools and methods of producing the means of life. Realising these changes gives greater possibilities for real life, instead of a bitter, uncertain struggle for mere existence, ever menaced by the danger of war. We see the oppressed peoples in the colonies, the proletariat in the industrial countries, the overwhelming majority of humanity struggling – struggling up the hillside, towards the dawn of Socialism. We see them slipping, falling, rising, even advancing towards their objective, led by great figures in advance, but ever alongside the marchers. Great figures like Wat Tyler, John Ball, Sir Thomas Moore, Gerald Winstanley, Edward Carpenter, Ruskin, Mathew Arnold, Keir Hardie, Tom Mann, Gallacher, Pollitt and Campbell.

We see the slaves in revolt, the serfs in rebellion, the handicapped men, bewildered but mute in us. The wage slaves striking the enclosures, the Bread Riots, the Luddites and the builders of Socialism. We know that all roads lead to Communism. We know the peoples of China, Russia, Bulgaria, Poland, Hungary and the other countries have taken this road and are holding out a helping hand to us. Marxism, Leninism, have been confirmed as true by history and this is a sure guarantee that Capitalism with its hateful exploitation and threat of wars without end will be smashed and replaced by a world-wide system of society which will assure to everyone the guarantee of the fullest possible development of all human faculties and permanent peace, prosperity and progress.

Robert Selkirk, 7th July 1951

JOE HILL, Union agitator and organiser in America was shot by a firing squad in 1915. Nationwide campaigns failed to stop American authorities from doing so. Joe Hill's "Preacher and a Slave" is sung to a hymn, "Sweet Bye and Bye". It was usually sung on long hunger marches in the thirties on their march to London. This is it.

> *Long haired Preachers come out every night*
> *Try to tell you what's wrong and what's right*
> *But when asked 'bout somethin' to eat*
> *They will answer with voices so sweet*
> *You will eat bye and bye*
> *In the glorious land above the sky*
> *Work and pray, live on hay*
> *You'll get pie in the sky*

When you die.
If you fight hard for children and wife
Try to get something good in this life
You'r a sinner and bad mean they say
When you die, you will sure go to Hell
Working men of all countries unite
Side by side we for freedom will fight
When the world and its wealth we have gained
To the bosses we'll sing this refrain

You will eat bye and bye
When you've learned how to cook and fry
Chop some wood t'will do you good
And you will eat in the sweet bye and bye

CHAPTER EIGHT
FIFE COMMUNIST PARTY

A brief outline of development

It is no accident that Fife should have a Communist M.P. and that the first president of the powerful Scottish area of the National Union of Mineworkers should be a Fife Communist.

The traditional militancy and readiness for sustained organised struggle in the Fife workers made inevitable the election of William Gallacher M.P. for West Fife and Abe Moffat to prominent positions, where their outstanding qualities of leadership could be used to best advantage of the workers.

Before the opening of this century of social upheaval, socialist pioneers were active in Fife, zealously propagating, despite victimisation and consequent semi-starvation, the urgent need to discard the harmful jungle principle of profit-making. They timelessly explained by meetings and literature on how profit-making must lead to poverty, degradation and war.

These early fighters for socialism did not only act as propagandists, they were the leaders in the class struggle in numerous bitterly fought industrial disputes, in forming and functioning of co-operation societies, in battles to secure the return of working class representation to councils, education authorities and parliament, so that enough decent houses might be built, pit-head baths erected, higher pensions secured, better educational facilities provided and improved public health services introduced.

These pioneers in carrying out the above mentioned herculean tasks, formed socialist, labour, communist and free-thought and anti-war organisations.

Under the influence of men like Keir Hardie and John McLean, they build live branches of Parties such as the Social Democrat Federation, Socialist Labour Party, I.L.P., Freethinkers League and so on, but their political activities were always closely linked with the mass day-to-day struggles.

Such was the historical, ideological and practical preparation for the formation of branches of the Communist Party in Fife. This preparation could only have been carried out by men like the pioneers, who did not hesitate to run the risk of losing jobs and were always ready to sacrifice leisure in the fight for social progress. In every village, town, pit, factory, farm and workshop the sacred spirit of resistance to oppression and the undying desire for real freedom were manifested daily.

It would indeed require many volumes to record even a part of the story of the courageous defiance of the greedy, grasping, reactionary employing and profit-making class by these early pioneers in the fight for a decent civilisation.

1921–1926

Members of the Communist Party played a leading part in the troublesome times following wholesale attacks by the employing class on wages when the post-war boom collapsed. The miners, supported by the rank and file of the other Trade Unions, despite the betrayal of the leaders of the Triple Alliance, resisted the attack. They had learned the main lessons of the 1894 Scottish Strikes and the 1912 British Miners Strike and they adopted a much more realistic attitude towards the conduct of the 1921 strike. Safety men were withdrawn from the pits, often as a result of mass action, despite the mobilisation of large forces of specially selected police.

Typical of the mood of the Miners were the events at Cowdenbeath, where huge demonstrations forcibly drew the fires which supplied power to the pumps and cages. Large scale battles with the police were common and the strikers, during one such battle, smashed shop windows and carried off the necessities which they required. Heavy sentences were imposed on the militant miners arrested at the time, but this did very little towards damping down the militancy of the miners, nor did the mass unemployment and victimisation which resulted from the defeat of the miners.

Charges to pay

_____d.

VED

POST OFFICE

TELEGRAM

No. 84

OFFICE STAMP

Prefix. Time handed in. Office of Origin and Service Instructions. Words.

WB461/68> The Harry Pollitt

UKFM 3. 27

26.1.30

At_____m

From_____

By_____

At_____m

To_____

By_____

Bob Selkirk 4 Tervis Place Cowdenbeath

Greetings from Captain and crew
Harry Pollitt sailing from Leningrad
to London. z.v. John Gallan
Brian Pollitt Peter Kerrigan
Nikolaj Matkovsky

For free repetition of doubtful words telephone "TELEGRAMS ENQUIRY" or call, with this form
at office of delivery. Other enquiries should be accompanied by this form, and, if possible, the envelope.

B or C

COMMUNIST PARTY
COWDENBEATH BRANCH

Councillor ROBERT SELKIRK

—

Three Year Plan

Unemployed workers in Kirkaldy made history during this period by their "Lawless Attack" on Parish Councillors, making them prisoners in their own Chambers until concessions were granted. The unemployed struggles throughout the industrial part of Fife forced the local authorities to raise scales, grant food and clothing to necessitous school children and start a few work schemes.

These concession certainly contributed toward preventing the undermining of public health. Branches of the National Unemployed Workers Committee Movement formed in this period, secured the support of Trade Unions, Labour Parties, Co-operative Societies and was instrumental in building a United Front against the reactionaries. For example, the mass march of the Rosyth unemployed represented every section of the movement and won certain demands from the local authority.

In 1921, on the initiative of Lumphinnans Miners Branch, whose members were sick of the continual surrender of the Right Wing leaders to every demand made by the Coalowners, the Reform Union was formed and soon had enrolled as members the majority of Fife miners. The division of the miners into two camps, the "Reform" and the "Old Union" had very detrimental effects, but there can be no doubt the policy of the live Reform Union forced the Old Union officials to adopt a much more militant attitude towards the wage-cutting coalowners, and led to a new interest in Union affairs. The "MINER", a half-penny paper published by the Reform Union had a weekly circulation of 17,000 and recruiting campaigns were continuous and embraced the whole coalfield.

The main task, however, of the Communist Party members in 1925 and the early part of 1926 was preparation for the gigantic struggle which lay ahead for the General Strike. It was comparatively easy to make workers aware of the issues involved in defence of the working class standards, because Baldwin, the Tory Prime Minister had said "The wages of all workers must come down" Sir James Lithgow, Lord Weir and other hard-baked Tories had also expressed the same idea on different occasions and in this case fore-warned was indeed fore-armed.

On top of all this Winston Churchill had made numerous bloodthirsty speeches calling his class to struggle in defence of profits. He appealed to his fellow exploiters to join the O.M.S., the Organisation for Maintenance of Supplies, a blacklegging organisation composed of those with fascist ideas concerning the use of violence to keep the masses in misery for the benefit of parasites.

Scores of meetings were held. Hundreds of resolutions were passed by Trade Union Branches, Trades Councils etc., calling on the miners. Thousands of leaflets were distributed containing a fighting lead and the circulation of the Communist Party weekly paper went up by leaps and bounds, especially after the imprisonment of the Central Committee of the Party.

When, despite the grovelling of the Right Wing leaders, the General Strike was declared, the mass response in Fife was beyond all expectations. For the nine days of the General Strike, the Fife workers were on top of the world. Through their Trades Councils and their Strike Committees they controlled the distribution and transportation of food and coal.

Possibly the Methil Trades Council had the most efficient organisation for these purposes and for mass picketing of miners to stop blacklegging, but all the Fife Trades Councils did a marvellous job, and were obviously being transformed into Councils of Action.

After the betrayal of the General Strike by the Right Wing leaders, the miners were left to fight alone. All the other strikers being ordered back to work by their weak-kneed leaders. Workers now flocked into the Fife Communist Party. It was so clear that our national leaders had been arrested because their policy was correct and that their courage was in glaring contrast to the cowardice of the Labour and Trade Union leaders. It was so evident that the Communists were in the forefront of the struggle, on the picket lines, in the campaign against black-legs, in the raising of money for soup kitchens, and in putting the miners case to non-mining sections of the communists and accruing support for demands of the Miners' Federation, summed up in the slogan "NOT A MINUTE ON THE DAY. NOT A PENNY OFF THE PAY".

The miners struggled heroically for six long months. After the miners had been on strike for several month, the Right Wing leaders emerged from their hiding places in order to propagate defeatism. "Never again will we strike" was their cry, which was naturally given great publicity in the Press. The Capitalist press reached unprecedented depths of falsehood. Police terrorism was intensified and many weaklings showed signs of returning to the pits on the owners harsh terms.

The Fife miners were the last to go back. Demonstrations against black-legs, which landed many strikers in the Sheriff Court, were organised after most areas had started work.

It was near the end of the strike that Right Wing defeatism, police terrorism and capitalist press lies reached the highest peak. Miners' MP's campaigned for a "breakaways" and the police in Lochore, Glencraig, Lochgelly, Valleyfield etc. employed the methods associated with the "Black and Tans". These were thugs used by the British Government to crush the Irish people. Batons were freely used and strikers arrested on the slightest pretext. Still the Fife miners held firm and returned to work as one body.

The Fife coalowners refused to employ those who had been active in the strike. They forced men from one village to work in the pit nearest another village to break up the solidarity of the miners, but hundreds of miners and their womenfolk replied by joining the Communist Party, and the morale of the Fife coalfield remained very high.

1926–1931

Experience during the past period had developed the capacity for leadership in the Fife Communists. A strong District Committee was functioning and a full time organiser had been appointed. One of the first tests was a ballot for the official position in the Scottish Miners Union. In the interests of unity the Reform Union had been liquidated and this meant the Communist Miners were in the Old Union and eligible for nomination. The result surprised the reactionaries, Smillie, Adamson and all the "old gang" were defeated and a Communist elected. It seems strange in those days of the "Witch Hunts" to recall that the campaign run by the party in these elections was organised around the slogans "VOTE FOR THE COMMUNIST NOMINEES". "VOTE FOR THE COMMUNIST INTERNATIONAL"

Unfortunately, Adamson, Smillie and company did not act like democrats and refused to abide by the results of the ballots. Adamson formed a break-away Union in Fife and this Union was recognised as the official Union by the Right Wing leadership of the British Miners Federation. Again the Fife miners were divided into two camps and the militants were forced to form the United Mineworkers of Scotland until 1936. This Union led every struggle of the Scottish miners against worsening conditions and put a brake on the plans of the blood-sucking coalowners.

In 1927 the Communists broke through into local government bodies. A Left-wing block, including three Communists, secured the majority on Lochgelly Town Council and made great headway in the building of houses by Direct Labour.

A Left-wing block of ten candidates, including two Communists were elected to Fife Education Authority and were instrumental in restricting the use of the strap, getting free school meals of higher quality for many children, by exposing the attempts of religious reactionaries to exploit the schools. Communists were elected to half a dozen school management committees and several school strikes were organised. One such strike in the Cowdenbeath district forced the granting of May Day as an annual holiday for the schools. Communists were returned to Wemyss, Culross, Ballingry and other Parish Councils. This led to increased scales of relief and much more humane treatment of unemployed and sick applicants for assistance. These councils were threatened with surcharges for paying more than the permitted scales, but they successfully defied this intimidation and forced the government to make the higher scales legal.

Following the election of many Communists to Institute Committees a real fight was organised against the dead hand of the Welfare Committee who opposed a progressive policy in the localities.

From 1928, many large scale marches to London, Glasgow, Cupar, Edinburgh and Dundee were organised. The marches forced concessions from "the powers that be", but even more important, they did much to counteract the harmful pernicious propaganda of the Right Wing leaders. The essence of this disarming anti-working class propaganda was "....do not demonstrate, do not march, do not strike, vote and leave it to us".

These marches brought into the open the strong desire of the rank and file for United Action. Everywhere the marches went they received mass support despite official Trade Union, Labour Party and Government bans. Co-operative Societies usually contributed generously to march funds and collections always more than met the expenditure involved in helping to keep several hundred men on the road, in the case of London marches, for several weeks on end. The marches were organised around the realistic and prophetic slogan "AGAINST HUNGER, FASCISM AND WAR", and naturally around the bitter hostility of reactionaries. The Fife County Council did everything to prevent the unemployed participating in the marches. They even had married men marchers arrested for "Wife Desertion", but the marchers appealed to the High Court and got the verdict in favour of the "Right to fight for better conditions for themselves and dependents".

The verdict of history must be that the marches put a strong, effective brake on the war-mongering fascists attempts to use the unemployed armies to lower wages and worsen the living conditions of the workers. In Fife the National Unemployed Workers Movement, led by members of the Communist Party, organised the marches, defended the unemployed at Courts of Referees, in Public Assistance Offices and against evictions from houses.

1931 saw the downfall of the second Labour Government, brought down by the cracking of the whip by the American financiers (just as they are doing under the Marshall Plan agreement), and by the failure of the Right Wing leaders to answer the American financiers by carrying out Socialist measures. Most workers had thought that the Right Wing leaders had learned their lesson of the failure of the 1924 Labour Government, but it was again demonstrated that Social Democrats always supported capitalism while talking socialism. The 1924, like the 1931 Government failed because of their policy of "....making capitalism work at the expense of the workers", but the mass resentment when they arrested J.R. Campbell for expressing working class sentiment was the immediate cause of their resignation.

These repeated betrayals; the Triple Alliance in 1921; the two Labour Governments; the General Strike; the liquidation of the Anglo Committee and the disorganisation of the unemployed struggles – all these destroyed the faith of thousands of militant workers in the Labour Movement, making it much more difficult to build a revolutionary party. But the Communist Party did continue to increase its membership.

The Government, while forced to restore the cuts, used every method of repression and many members of the Communist Party were sent to prison for their part in the fight. United Front Committees were formed in the industrial parts of Fife. Even Labour MPs actively participated in the work of organising huge marches and demonstrations. Several pit strikes against wage cuts and worsening of work conditions were led by the U.M.S.. The strike of the Valleyfield miners was a keenly fought dispute and aroused intense interest throughout the country.

1931–39

This period was dominated by the evidence of hunger among wide sections of the people, the rapid rise of fascism and the growing danger of war. The National Government carried out the instructions of the American financiers in order to get a loan and made sweeping cuts in wages and unemployed benefits. The mass struggle against these attacks reached unprecedented heights and led to united mass action by unemployed workers, civil servants, teachers and professional workers. The current spread to the Navy and cold shivers ran down the spine of reactionaries when the reliable "Jack Tar" mutinied at Invergordon.

All this intense activity prepared the ground for the 1935 General Election and Gallacher was returned to Parliament for West Fife. In addition, more Communists were returned to County, Town and District Councils and more workers joined the Party.

The Fife Party collected hundreds of pounds and much foodstuffs for the struggling Spanish workers who had been treacherously attacked in 1936 by Franco, Hitler and Mussolini and found themselves deserted by the Right Wingers in other countries. Fife sent its quota of volunteers to the International Brigade and some courageous Fife Comrades made the supreme sacrifice in Spain. It is worth recalling that slogans white-washed on Fife roads in 1936-37 correctly stated that "Bombs on Madrid means bombs on London" and "Appeasement of Hitler means Second World War".

It is clear the Fife Party played a big part in the fight to prevent war. Our members were also in the lead for campaigning for bomb-proof shelters, while other parties opposed these proposals and cunning contractors reaped a golden harvest electing shelters which gave next to no protection against bombs and wardens dreaded the prospect of a real blitz in their district. In every phase of air raid precautions services our party members were active, doing their utmost to defend the people.

The beginning of the war, made inevitable by Chamberlain's policy of appeasement of Hitler, supported by everyone except our party members and supporters, again recalled the power of the Capitalist press to mislead people. Readers were informed – and many believed – that "Munich Agreement Will Save World Peace", that the Red Army is useless, it has no modern equipment, it cannot beat the small Finnish Army. Later it was asserted that : "....the Nazi Army will go through the Red Army like a hot knife through butter", but actually the Red Army stopped and defeated 75 per cent of Hitler's armies. Only when the Red Army forced the Nazi Army back hundreds of miles did the Allied military leaders agree to open the second front. These militarists, because of their prejudice against Russia, broke the promise to launch the second front in 1942. They even opposed sending military equipment to the Red Army on the grounds that "....anything sent will be captured and used by the Germans".

After it was clear the Red Army would beat the German Fascist Army, Churchill stated "No other government could have survived the heavy shock of the German attack. No other army could have done the job done by the Red Army".

However, Churchill and the other critics of the Red Army act in the most brazen fashion; though they have been proved 100 per.cent. wrong in their criticism, they still, in the most shameless fashion, broadcast slanderous statements concerning the Red Army and the Soviet Union. They are given space in the Press, facilities on the BBC, assistance from hundreds of pulpits, to circulate continuously every lie invented by fascist beasts, and Churchill apparently thinks "his armies" can succeed where Hitler's armies failed.

During the war against Fascism, after those who wanted the "war against Fascism switched to a war against Communism" had been defeated and removed from power, the Fife communists were outstanding in their efforts to increase production. This made them temporarily unpopular, but now it is recognised on all hands, the increased production was necessary and in the best interests of the working class.

With the ending of the war, Gallacher was returned to Parliament,

Abe Moffatt was elected by the Scottish Miners as their President, and the Fife Party have organised campaigns on Housing, Rents, Wages, Pensions, Peace and other issues directly affecting the well-being of the people. The keynote of all the campaigns was "Prevent a Tory come-back by getting the Labour Government to carry out its General Election Programme".

The continuous campaign since 1945 against increase in housing rents has been successful in preventing increases, in modifying the amount of increase, in placing the main responsibility for increases on the Government for failing to control the big monopolies, combines and manufacturing building materials.

The sustained campaign for the proper utilisation of the Rosyth Dockyard has been effective in preventing the criminal waste of national resources and unemployment.

The Fife Party published a "Plan for Fife Prosperity" and several copies of "Gallacher's "Gazette"; organised conferences, discussions, education classes and produced many leaflets and Press statements. No other M.P. has addressed more constituency meetings than Gallacher, and no organisation has attended to more grievances than the Communist Party. The "Gallacher's Gazette" proved to be as popular as the Pit and Factory papers issued in 1929–35; papers with revealing titles like the "Torch", "Lamp", "Flame", "Searchlight", "Bomb", "Mash", "Crowpicker", "Panbolt", "Red Guard", "Double Unit" etc. These papers helped the "Daily Worker" in its task of mobilising the people for struggle against man's misery, fascism and war. Persons who are seriously concerned with the necessary struggle for Socialism must be regular readers of the "Daily Worker", the only paper owned by the working class of the country.

There can be no doubt that Fife Communists can be proud of their role in the fight against reaction. There ought to be no question of any unprejudiced person refusing to join the Communist Party. This is the Party which will lead the workers to the establishment of socialism. Full blooded socialism will banish the root cause of man's misery – fascism and war. The Communist Party leads the fight for peace and this is the most important struggle for our generation. JOIN THE COMMUNIST PARTY.

CHAPTER NINE
EXTRACTS FROM COWDENBEATH COMMUNIST PARTY TOWN COUNCIL MONTHLY BULLETIN
Editor Bob Selkirk

In 1946 Councillor Selkirk moved that the Town Council should form a Housing Department with a full-time Housing Manager to make a real sustained drive to build the thousand houses that were actually required in Cowdenbeath. This motion was defeated by eight votes to three with only the three Communist Councillors voting for the Motion. Bailie Selkirk, Councillor Sharp and Councillor Campbell. The majority voted for Mr C.A. Alexander continuing as Housing Manager, responsible for repairs and maintenance of eight hundred houses and planning and building of one thousand houses. This was to be a spare time job for Mr Alexander, his other jobs being as follows:

- Sanitary Inspector, Beath District County Council;
- Joint Town Clerk;
- Clerk and Assessor to the Licensing Court;
- Dean of Guild Court and Police Court;
- Clerk to the Local Pensioners' Committee;
- Administration of Statutes;
- Supervision of Roads, Sewers and Buildings;
- Preparation of plans for same and supervision of all works involved;
- Preparation of Reports and Inspector of places of public entertainment;
- Master of Works to the Dean of Guild Court;
- Supervision of Slaughterhouses, British Restaurants, Public Park and Conveniences;
- Water Engineer;
- Sanitary Inspector;
- Supervision of General Sanitation of the Burgh;

- Administration of Public Health Statutes including Housing Acts, Infectious diseases;
- Meat Inspection and work under Food and Drug Mart;
- Cleansing Inspector, supervising cleansing of all streets etc;
- Removal and disposal of refuse and collection of salvage;
- Lighting Inspector, supervision of street lighting, also back court lighting;
- Shops Inspector. Administration of Shops Act;
- Housing Maintenance;
- Supervision of all Town Council Houses for repair and maintenance;
- Housing supervision and preparation of new schemes, including Layout, and Type Plan Schedules and execution of Schemes.

How is it possible for Mr Alexander to give the time to take all the problems involved, Surveying, Planning, Preparation of Schedules, Arranging Contracts, Securing of Materials, Approaching all the separate Government Departments concerned in the Housing etc?

What can you do?

This position cannot be permitted to continue, we must get houses quickly. We must realise that health is being undermined by deplorable housing conditions. We must realise that scores of young people are being robbed of a fair chance of happiness by having to live in sub-lets. The Communist Party is determined to do all it can to get the Housing Department with a full-time Housing Manager. You can assist by letting the Councillor know that you support this common sense proposal. Raise it with the Council. Raise it within your organisation. Write to the local press and write to your local M.P. Write to the Medical Officer, County Buildings, Cupar, or the Department of Health, St Andrews House, Edinburgh. We must have a drive for houses.

Sewerage scandal

Cesspools of sewerage are in evidence in the Perth Road area, especially in the south of Lumphinnans School and to the south of Central Cooking Depot in Broad Street. As a result of recent protests by the Communist Councillors too much attention has been drawn to these sources of disease, but not much has been done in the way of actually finding a remedy for these blots on the reputation of Cowdenbeath. South West of the Cooking Depot, there is a sewerage pipe which has been affected by subsidence and the level of the pipe altered, now the sewerage does not run inside the pipe as originally intended, but in the open burn alongside. There are many deep pools in the burn and the rest can be left to the imagination and sense of smell. This sewerage pipe will serve the four hundred new houses to be built at West Broad Street site and this matter must be tackled right away. It, like many other things, has been neglected too long. The health of the people must be safeguarded.

CHAPTER TEN
THE PARTY

We have to assume that every comrade present has read the Study Theme on Pollitt's "Peace Depends on the People" which has been issued by our Central Committee.

In the Study Theme we are informed that the need for the Party was recognised as a result of the experiences of the workers in their organised struggles against the Capitalist Class. That is to say the Party is the inevitable development of all the past class struggles of all the progressive and revolutionary trends of mankind throughout the ages.

To deal adequately with the Role of the Party which could obviously not be done within the limits of the Study Theme, it would be necessary to delve deeply into all past history. We would have to examine the outline and detail of all the economic, political and social conditions which gave rise to the mighty Slave Revolts, the widespread Peasants Revolts, the pioneers of our Trade Unions, Co-operative and Labour Movement. It might make this discussion more interesting if we dealt with the lives of the John Balls, Wat Tylers, the Levellers, the Chartists, who personified the struggle of the masses against class oppression, but the comrades who take seriously the advice of the Central Committee on the essential need for self study can peruse the classics on the historical roots of the Party.

(Quotation from Communist Review on Self Study)

ANCIENT SOCIETY by Morgan, SIX CENTURIES OF WORK AND WAGES by Rogers, TOWN AND COUNTRY LABOUR by Hammond, INDUSTRIAL HISTORY by Gibbins, CONDITIONS OF THE ENGLISH WORKING CLASSES by Engels, POST WAR HISTORY OF THE BRITISH WORKERS by Hutt and some of the historical studies by Childe or the PEOPLES HISTORIES by Hill or Morton, or some of the historical novels like THE ENGLISH EPISODE by Poulsen.

However, the reading materials given in our Study Theme are:

LEFT WING COMMUNISM by Lenin, LENIN ON BRITAIN, and Stalin on the PARTY AND FOUNDATIONS OF LENINISM.

It is indeed fortunate for the success of our struggle that we have not had to wend our weary way through all the classics mentioned above, because Marx, Engels, Lenin and Stalin, have given us the benefit of their almost unbelievable capacity for study and generalisation.

Lenin tells us that "Marx continued and completed the work of the German philosophers, the French social revolutionaries and the English economists".

When one contemplates the ponderous volumes of the German philosophers, the lengthy and brilliant works of the French Iconoclasts, the intricacies of the verbose treatises of the British economists – it is indeed staggering to imagine one man analysing and generalising all these works – but Marx did this in his "Materialist Conception of History", the most brilliant generalisation of all past, present and future, is sufficient proof.

Lenin continued and completed for his period the great work of Marx, and Stalin has done his job for the work of Lenin and so we can start today on the basis of Stalin's "Foundations of Leninism".

In "Foundations of Leninism" Stalin finds it necessary to deal with the Historical Roots of Leninism – Marxist method – Marxist theory – Dictatorship of the proletariat – Peasant problem – the National problem – Strategy and Tactics – before the ground is prepared for the Party.

We cannot deal in this way with the Party and so we must take some significant quotations from this booklet:

"Matters have changed radically with the dawn of the new period. The new period is one of open class collisions, of revolutionary action by the proletariat, of proletarian revolution, a period when forces are being mustered for the overthrow of Imperialism and the seizure of power by the proletariat".

"Formerly the proletariat revolution was regarded exclusively as the result of the internal development of a given country. Now this point of view is no longer adequate. Now the proletarian revolution can be regarded as the result of the development of the contradictions within the world system of Imperialism, as the result of the snapping of the chain of the Imperialist world front in one country or another".

"Stalin also says '.....that in the fight against Imperialism the old parties, Trade Unions, Co-operatives have been proved helpless in face of never-ending capitalist attacks and the workers are faced with the necessity to build a new type of Party' , – the Leninist Party built on the principles worked out by Lenin.

These quotations give the key note struck by our Study Theme.

CHAPTER ELEVEN
POLICE RESPONSE

A mass deputation on the evening of my eviction to the Co-operative Board was dispersed by a baton charge on his orders. But at a later demonstration the next evening was not dispersed because the demonstrators had pick shafts etc., and anyone giving the orders for a baton charge was likely to get hurt and Inspector Clark avoided any possibility of this happening.

Time ran on and Inspector Clark had to retire. The County Council wanted his house for his successor and tried to evict him. On hearing of this I posted a letter to him offering to organise his defence, but he did not accept my offer.

Agitators

Inspector Clark of Lochgelly seemed to hate the working class fighters for social justice. He showed his hatred in many ways by applying his shoulder in such a way that the agitator passing him on the pavement when few people were about, found himself flung on to the street or by trying to step on to the fingers of the agitator chalking slogans on the roadway. He did this thing to me and on one occasion when he arrested me after an eviction fight, he provoked me with an escort of six policemen, a sergeant and Inspector Clark. This was to create the impression that I was a dangerous criminal.

Somewhat later, when I was evicted, not because of rent arrears, but because the local Tory minded Co-operative Board alleged that they needed my house for the extension of premises, he gave the order for two policemen to hold my arms, while another policeman gave me what is known as the "rabbit punch" or stupifying blows on the back of the neck.

Moscow Gold

At one period the police in Fifeshire were convinced that leaders of the Unemployed Movement were receiving some of the Moscow Gold sent by the Russian Workers to help the striking miners of 1926. Inspector White of Lochgelly imagined that I was receiving the Moscow Gold. He arrested me and took me to the Police Station and questioned me as to my income. I had just managed to scrape up three pence for an ounce of tobacco. I had just bought it before he arrested me. During the questioning I started to laugh at the idea of not being able to smoke the tobacco. The Inspector thought that I was laughing at him and he flung me out of the Police Station. I then enjoyed the first smoke for several days.

A letter to the 'Daily Worker'
6th October 1944

Dear Comrade,

The key question for the British Workers at the moment is "How to secure the reorganisation of the Labour Cabinet so as to replace the Right Wings by Socialists who will carry out a realistic class policy for the solution of the class"?

Only when this urgent task has been accomplished, will it be sensible to expect the speedy and wholehearted operation of such measures as the drastic reduction of Armed Forces, profits and prices, the drafting of a realistic overall economic plan, the negotiating of trade agreements with the colonies, dominions, Soviet Union and European countries, the discharging of Churchill on foreign policy etc.

What steps can the Left take to secure such reorganisation of the Cabinet?

It seems pretty obvious we ought to be in the position to name the Socialist M.P. we desire to be our Cabinet Minister. The reactionaries want Bevin as Prime Minister. Who is our choice for Prime Minister?

The reactionaries use all their industrial and political power to secure support for Bevin. When, where, how should the Left operate to counter these moves and secure the Cabinet changes we recognise as vital and urgent?

Are we consciously using our industrial power to solve the "key problem" or are we simply "campaigning in general" for a working class solution to the crisis?

Yours fraternally,
Robt Selkirk
Cowdenbeath.

CHAPTER TWELVE
ON PEACE

Women and peace

It seems to me that there are several things that we must do in order to secure the leadership of the mass fight against the war-mongers. First, we have to convince the people that the American warmongers are responsible for the present war danger. Second, we have to convince them that the Labour Government is absolutely subservient to the American war-mongers. Third, we must convince them that there is no chance of averting war, improving living standards, regaining our national independence or moving towards Socialism unless the policy of Atlee, Bevin and Co is changed. Fourth, we must convince them that the mass action of the people can prevent war.

In these urgent tasks, the Party obviously must win the support of the women-folk. More effort must be made to recruit women and draw them into the work of the Party.

In Fife, nearly a third of the members are women, but only one or two attend area Committee or Branch meetings. It is clear that this can only lead to most of our efforts not getting the full results required in the present situation.

We actually have a position where some Branch leaders feel they have no responsibility for Womens' Sections. They think this is a job for the women members. In Cowdenbeath we have a Womens' Section which has done a lot of real work in the fight for Peace and the raising of finance.

Anti-Nuclear Campaign

Shortly after the conclusion of the 1939-45 war I proposed to the General Secretary, Harry Pollitt that the E.C. should consider forming a department with the special task of replying to anti-Soviet slanders. It seemed to me that the cold war was like a poisonous stream infecting with reactionary ideas the mass of the population.

I knew that from its inception the USSR had made the running for social advance and world peace. It now seems to me that our position as a Communist Party would have been much stronger if the suggestion had been accepted by the E.C.

When Kruschev proposed at the United Nations a plan for Total Dis-armament, I again proposed to the E.C. that we should make the fight for dis-armament our main task. I made the suggestion because I believed this proposal made by the Soviet Union was vitally important to humanity, because it was obvious the Cold War must lead to the "hot" nuclear war.

It appeared to me that this was an aim which would appeal to the overwhelming majority of the people and so lay the basis for a broad united front against reaction. Many years afterwards I remained convinced that this would have been the correct policy. A few years ago I wrote to John Gollan, General Secretary, with this proposal, that a Commission should be formed to go thoroughly into the reasons for our lack of progress as a Party. It has never been made public that the French Party, with a mass membership, has recognised the need to form a Commission to investigate as to how their methods of propaganda can be improved. Undoubtedly, if this is needed in the case of the French Party, it is absolutely essential in the case of the British Party where membership remains static.

CHAPTER THIRTEEN
THE PENSIONERS' MOVEMENT

Bob Selkirk, as well as being a member of Cowdenbeath Town Council for 32 years with all that involved, and a member of the Board of Management of the Co-operatives Society, formed a branch of The Old Age Pensioners Association to fight for higher pensions. The Association was always busy with one campaign after another, bringing pressure on the Government and getting involved in the Unions to get support for their demand for higher pensions.

His ability was soon recognised and when the opportunity arose he became Scottish Secretary of the Association as well as Editor of their paper, 'The Scottish Pensioner', which was a monthly paper, sold by the Branches, some of which had quite a big sale. The paper had quite a bit of work involved in getting it ready for the printer. The Branches sent in reports of their activity throughout the month, as well as letters from the members to the Editor. Any new anomalies and further activities were explained by Bob as the Editor.

A certain date each month he had to design each page of the 'Pensioner'. I used to like to help him put it together for the printer. Material from the Branches or members was not always straightforward. Some reports or letters had to be added to or reduced or even rewritten, depending on the space available. One time Bob's trip to Russia coincided with getting the paper ready for the printer. I agreed to do the paper that month for him if he wrote the Editorial column for me – which he did.

When he returned from his visit to Russia he gave me 10 out of 10 marks for my production of the paper and offered me the job. Of course I did not take it. I was still working to a Boss.

The Annual Conference of the Scottish Old Age Pensioners Associ-

THE SCOTTISH PENSIONER

Official Organ of the Scottish Old Age Pension Association

No. 156   JANUARY, 1961   Price 2d

INTO ACTION NOW!

E.C. REPORT

HELPING OLD FOLK

THE General Secretary reported receipt of acknowledgment from Secretary for Scotland of our request for an interview on pensions and N.A.B. scales, but only a promise to place the matter before Mr Maclay at some appropriate time.

B.B.C. WON'T PLAY

A letter from the B.B.C. refuses us time on the air to put our case, excuse being that "pensions are not topical at the moment" and some "free lances" had recently aired their views on the problem. Five million old folk and their millions of ardent supporters will feel amazement at this assertion that pensions are not topical all the time. The "chappie" who sent reply does not know pensioners must be active all the time and look on "free lances" as football fans would look on "free players" who claimed they were entitled to "kick into any goal."

THEY HIT THE POOREST

The President in a "hit the politicians" speech urged the E.C. members to intensify activities to force the Government to adopt a favourable attitude and persuade the Government to pay pensions in

GREAT ACTIVITY

Mr Hughes told the E.C. about invitations sent to Mr Thomson and Mr Strachey, local M.P.'s, to speak at meetings; but Mr Strachey had not replied and Mr Thomson had at least replied. He also reported efforts Area Council had made to make the function for Dundee Printers a success.

Mr Stewart reported on a whole lot of steps taken by Glasgow Area Council, including letters to Prime Minister and others "in authority over us. He indicated our thanks were due to M.P.'s and others who had supported our demands. Police Judge Paterson reported the overcoming of local difficulties in the way of building the Association in the Burdens.

Mrs Flockhart told E.C. of the prospects in Longniddrie and North Berwick for branch activity, and Mrs Worsley gave a clear report on the efforts to increase activity of Lanarkshire Area Council and the improved situation in Carluke and other branches.

Mr McCue affirmed the determination of Midlothian Area Council to bring

The Big "Freeze" and Pensions

There have been many Press reports of increased death rate among pensioners during severe wintry weather.

Medical Officers have made public their opinion that many of these deaths were due to Hypothermia (extreme cold) caused by insufficiency of nourishing food and inadequate supply of fuel and warm clothing.

A Prolonged "Freeze" for Pensioners

The last time pensions were increased was March, 1965. Since then prices have soared and the value of the increase wiped out. Wage-earners, unfortunately, are being threatened by a six months' freeze, but pensioners have already had an eighteen months' freeze of income, accompanied by " unfrozen " prices.

An Appeal

The Scottish Old Age Pensions Association under these dire circumstances appeal for the active support of all who wish to prevent thousands of our old folk enduring a tragic end to their period of retirement. Publicity for resolutions from Trade Unions, Co-operative Organisations and Political Parties will bring pressure on the Government for immediate increase in retirement pension rates.

Our Charter Demands

Many organisations have gone on record in support of our Charter. This Charter demands the payment of a pension of £5 per week per person.

This is the minimum required to secure justice for pensioners.

SUPPORT THE FIGHT FOR JUSTICE TO OUR OLD FOLK.

ation was held in a different part of Scotland every year. It was held in Aberdeen in about 1970. The Secretary of the Aberdeen Branch invited Bob to visit the Sheltered Accommodation they had been able to get the powers that be to build for their elderly in Aberdeen. He was impressed with what he saw and thought it would be very good for Cowdenbeath. He reported all about it at the next meeting of the Cowdenbeath Old Age Pensioners Branch, who were all very interested and agreed with him that he should raise it at the next Town Council meeting.

The Council were not interested at first, but he kept raising it at every opportunity. In the end he suggested that the Council should visit Aberdeen and see for themselves how advantageous it would be for Cowdenbeath's elderly citizens. This was done and the result was the first Sheltered House being built in Cowdenbeath in 1970, named 'Sunnyside Court', which was opened by Bob Selkirk.

That was the first of many more such houses being built in and around Cowdenbeath for the elderly over the years. People are living much longer than in the past and many more houses of that kind should be available in every area for the elderly. A lift has been added to Sunnyside Court which makes it more suitable for those unable to use the stairs. There is sheltered accommodation for a single person as well as for a married couple, with a warden on call day and night. Included in the rent is heating, a communal TV license and a laundry with washing machine. A home help service is available where necessary.

Bob Selkirk was very well liked as Secretary of the Old Age Pensioners Association and they were very sorry when he retired. They gave him a gift of money as their appreciation of him and he used the money to get his autobiography 'The Life of a Worker' published (see **Part Two**).

The Secretary of the English Pensioners was also sorry when Bob retired for he always kept him informed of the activities of the Scottish Pensioners so that they would both be fighting for the same demands at the same time.

In 1966 the Government gave pensioners a rise, but it was not to be paid till several months later. Bob wrote to the Minister of Pensions urging them to pay it right away, but they would not budge. By the time it would be paid many pensioners would have died, which they knew, so they saved that money. My Dad always said he would not get the increase. He died on the Wednesday and his pension was not due until the Thursday – the next day! He always said "Live horse and you'll get corn".

Mary Docherty

Call for One Day Strike to win higher pension

On Saturday 22nd September 1956, at a conference attended by 141 delegates from Town Councils, Trade Unions, Co-operative and Labour Movement; with two M.P.s, three doctors, General Secretary of the Scottish Miners, President of the Co-operative Womens' Guild on the platform; Provost Wright of Kirkcaldy proposed a campaign to get a One Day Strike of all workers to force this Tory Government to increase old age pensions.

The strong case for a One Day Strike can be summarised as follows:
1. Medical evidence proves that our old folk are seriously suffering from malnutrition and lack of comforts.
2. Everybody grows older and it is sound commonsense for everybody to fight for higher pensions.
3. The old folk built the Trade Union, Labour and Co-operative movements that won us the improvement in living conditions we have today.
4. This Tory Government has considerably increased the swollen incomes of the moneylenders, profiteers and armament combines.
5. The 'upper' class never in history wasted so much in luxurious living.
6. Thousands of resolutions and medical reports have failed to move this Government and so industrial action is required urgently to save lives. The pioneers of our Movement always said: "Use both hands, industrial and political, when you are fighting the Tory enemy".

It is hoped you and your organisation will help to win support for this worthwhile objective and so help the old folk of this generation.

Dr Cowan, Medical Officer for the Glasgow Area, said at the above conference, "The present treatment of the old folks is Murder of the Old Folks" and he knows the position.

Do not let us be described as accomplices of the 'cultured' murderers. Let us act now against the heartless parasites and politicians who deny justice to the old folk.

WE WANT JUSTICE – NOT CHARITY – ACT NOW!

Councillor Robert Selkirk
Cowdenbeath Branch
Communist Party

Report from the 'Daily Worker'

Some 250 old age pensioners from all over the North West London area demonstrated in Ealing (Middx) on Saturday 13th October in support of the national demand for a £3 a week pension.

In bright sunshine and carrying posters reading "You're a worker today, a pensioner tomorrow. This is your fight" and "Could you live on £2 a week?", they marched half a mile.

Cheerful and determined – that was the mood of these marchers. The very old were helped on their way by the not-so-old. A blind man leaned confidently on his neighbour's shoulder. A little girl lent a willing hand in supporting a heavy banner.

As they marched so did they sing. Making up their own words to the tune of "The Happy Wanderers: Could you live on £2 a week? Oh no, Oh no, Oh no" went the simple refrain.

They applauded loudly when Mrs M Nelson of the Western Area Council of Old Age Pensions Association said: "We are not prepared to sit at home and starve in silence."

And there was more applause when Councillor Mrs Grace Ainsley, Deputy Mayor of Ealing said: "I hope this afternoon is going to start the ball rolling for similar rallies all over London."

The support of the Trade Union Movement in the area was pledged by Mr C Lowings of Willesden No. 2 Branch of the Amalgamated Engineering Union. This was as much the workers' fight as it was that of the old people, he said.

Open letter to Sir Geoff Hutchinson

Sir,

We write to you, not as a person asking favours, but as a citizen seeking justice. Like Robert Burns, we know if we had been born in a mansion it would have been much easier to have a comfortable old age, but one does not choose to be born in a wee house, and so there are thousands seeking National Assistance who might have been life peers if only they had a choice of birthplace.

More than fifty years ago Lord Leverhulme said: "Everyone could have as high a standard of living as a Cabinet Minister if things were properly organised". During these fifty years the nation's capacity to produce food, clothing, shelter, luxuries, etc., has increased at least three times, and so it ought to be possible for everyone to have a standard of living equal to a multi-company director.

This is the background to this letter concerning certain specific grievances for which we hold the Board responsible. Of course, the columns of the 'Pensioner' are open for your defence of your enumeration of extenuating circumstances.

The Rent Rule

On 1st February 1957 you stated in a letter to an MP "I also referred to changes in the general level of rents especially as a result of Rent Act 1957, and it may be desirable for the Committees to consider the matter in the light of such changes when the full effect of the Act can be seen."

In March 1959, enough of the tragic results of the 1957 Rent Act can be seen to make the reconsideration of the local rent rules an urgent matter, especially when one takes into account the trickery which reduced the scales of your Board in relation to increased basic pension scales, and, so reduced the amount of assistance given to thousands of applicants, even those who had only been getting 6 shillings or less previously. The number on the Board was substantially reduced and then Tory spokesmen claimed this showed a big improvement in the position of the old pensioners.

Wage-earning Members

In your regulations you delude the public into believing that wage-earning members of the household of an applicant are only forced to pay 7 shillings per week towards the rent. This would be a fair rule as the working members of the family may be studying, may be contemplating marriage, may be intending to seek refuge in Australia or some other part of the world and requiring all their wages left after they augment the pension paid by your Government to their parents. However, your Board forces them in many cases to pay all the rent or a big part of the rent. The Family Means Test is operated.

Exceptional Needs

During the years of your Chairmanship of NAB there has been a rapid whittling away of the grants for exceptional needs. One case I have in mind is that of a mother of a big family whose family left the nest and she became a widow. She got married to another lonely old age pensioner and had her pension reduced from 50 shillings plus rent to 16 shillings per week because her second husband had a small pit pension and small increment for working three years after 65. The old couple banished loneliness but opened the door to malnutrition. They could not get relief of rates because your Board would have deducted relief from 16 shillings assistance.

Come Into the Open

We draw your attention to other critical articles in this issue and repeat our offer of space for your reply. We would welcome your defence so that we might use all the 'ammunition' we have accumulated during our period of retirement in a grateful country.

Faithfully yours,
THE EDITOR
Bob Selkirk

'The Scottish Pensioner' – *April 1959*
EDITOR'S COMMENTS

Many historical changes have taken place "in our time", progressive changes for which our generation have fought.

One sometimes hears younger people talking about "what we are doing for the old folk". It would be useful if oftener they thought of "what the old folk have done for them". The old folk of today have seen coming into existence, free school books, free milk and meals and clothing for necessitous school children: we played our part in establishing the right of Councils to build houses; the shorter working day; higher pensions; higher scales for the sick and unemployed .... etc.

We fought in two world wars to "save small nations from German militarism" and retain the right to live in "a land fit for heroes". Our struggles against bitter opposition laid the basis for the social advance made in 1945–48. No one can deny that if the employers had thought we would never strike they would never have paid higher wages.

First Time in History

During our time there has been formed the first permanent organisation of old folk to fight for social justice, and the success of our fight will be the measure of the advance towards better conditions for the young folk of today. Not so long ago it would have seemed absurd to suggest that old folk could organise and act on their own behalf in such a way as to make the authorities take notice, but the incredible has become reality.

Growing Influence

Our influence must grow because old folk are forming an even greater percentage of the population. With unity around clearly defined aims, we can be a growing force in deciding the results of elections. Our policy must be one that unites all the pensioners and does not antagonise the employed youngsters; a policy of higher pensions without any increase in the deductions from the pay packet. We must be against high prices because pensions always lag behind prices.

The Immediate Future

Talk of a General Election is in the air. Voters everywhere realise there is no sound economic reason for poverty in old age or any age. There is no excuse for a married couple getting less per head than a household composed of single persons. The reduction by the Tory Government of the Exchequer grant to Insurance Fund can be altered in twenty four hours by passing a Supplementary Estimate through the Houses of Parliament. We want the Government which will agree to raise the pensions to the level demanded by the Association.
R. Selkirk

Our aims in 1959
1. Basic pension of £3.10s per week per person; to increase with cost of living and no increase in contributions paid by employed persons.
2. Restoration of NAB scales and disregards raised to 1948 value and 1956 relation to basic pension.

3. Chiropody treatment free, cheap hot meals, home helps free of charge, old folks clubs with no membership fee, adequate hospital accommodation for old folk.
4. Old people's downstairs houses with all modern conveniences at low rents.

Objects

Branches, Area Councils, ECs to draw members into widespread activities in support of above demands. Activities to include sale of the 'Pensioner', heckling of candidates, interviews with MPs and Councillors, letters to the local press, recruiting of members to the Association. *R. Selkirk.*

CHAPTER FOURTEEN
INTERNATIONAL SOLIDARITY

Bob Selkirk was a visitor to the Soviet Union on four different occasions as well as one to Czechoslovakia. On each occasion he reported back where he had visited and what his impression was, what progress had been made and how he had been treated. On every occasion he could not fail to recognise the difference between a Capitalist system of society and a country whose economy was based on a Socialist system of society, a planned economy. Each time he was more and more impressed with the progress of the First Workers' Republic.

Before the Revolution, the vast majority of the population could neither read nor write. When I was in Russia in 1929 the school children were going home from school and teaching their parents and sometimes their grandparents to read and write, all to become good citizens of the First Workers' Republic.

After defeating Fascists the way they did and rebuilding their country as quickly as they did, it breaks my heart to see it as it is today.

People who have been on holiday to the Soviet Union, before what it became what it is today, cannot but admit that the Socialist system of society was being successful. One must not forget that the Red Army and the Soviet people had to beat off more than half the entire German Army and had to rebuild so many of their beautiful cities, plough up the land to sow their crops to feed their people, with no help from the Capitalist world around them. Many sacrifices had to be made and perhaps a few mistakes made which were taken advantage of to the detriment of the Soviet leaders.

But I am sure the Soviet Union will one day rise again and be The Union of Socialist Soviet Republics.

Mary Docherty

A visit to Czechoslovakia 1957

In 1957 Bob Selkirk made the first of his overseas visits. He submitted meticulous reports of his itinerary and experiences to the people of Cowdenbeath.

One can only expect to get space for a few of the new experiences met in a four weeks crowded visit. As one who can remember the pleasures got from a ride in a haycart for a few miles on the Sunday School Trip, my first new enjoyable experience was stepping on to a 'plane at Turnhouse. It flew at 319 miles per hour and rose to an altitude of 19,000 feet, and did the journey to London in less than one and a half hours. This gave just enough time to enjoy the splendid meal served on the 'plane to each passenger. then it was a case of boarding another 'plane for the flight to Brussels and after a somewhat longer wait, another 'plane for Prague in time for tea. Having taken less time than it would have been taken by train from Edinburgh to London, and feeling much less fatigue by 'plane travel than train travel.

One of the first things I noticed in Czechoslovakia was the hygienic dust carts, completely closed in and with a mechanical gadget for lifting the dustbins and emptying them without any dust flying about in the air. Several weeks afterwards we paid a visit to a synthetic oil works and were struck by the spectacle of huge tubes, carried on trestles, stretching away into the open country. Upon enquiry we were informed these tubes carried the fumes and dust away to waste ground where there were no houses. Everywhere we did go, we were struck by similar measures taken to prevent ill health. As one of the Medical Officers said to us. The emphasis here is on prevention of disease. At every pit and factory there is a Clinic and a fully trained Medical Staff.

At the first pit we visited there was a full-time Doctor and three Nurses. This is the number laid down by law for each 800 employees. The Clinic was equipped with X-ray and all other appliances required for the statutory medical check-up, every six months of every employee. If the check-up establishes that any employee is below par, the Trade Union is authorised to provide the necessary treatment, whether it be a change of job or a rest in the numerous workers' hostels in the mountains or spas free of charge to the patient. Whilst off work they receive 90 per cent of the average wage for the industry.

The children are not forgotten in the scheme of things. As a life-long advocate of the abolition of the instrument of uncivilised folk, "the strap", I was most pleased to find that it was illegal to use this outlet for sadistic traits. There is a system of mountain schools, where the whole school in an industrial area spends a month each year. During the winter months this period is cut down to ten days and the children are mainly involved, not in the usual lessons, but in winter sports such as skiing. One of the special treats for good work and behaviour in the summertime is for the whole class, except the badly behaved, to have a trip to the wonderful aerial railway which runs to the peak in the Tatra Mountain Range. It is over 8000 feet high from which a magnificent view is had. I have no doubt that the teachers of Czechoslovakia reach a very high standard in their training and sympathetic handling of children in their care. In support of this opinion, while not making any sweeping claims, I noticed certain things which reflect the good results from the education system.

One evening while sitting watching the dancers at an open-air dance garden, where all kinds of refreshments were served, the ladies left their handbags lying unprotected on their tables when they went up for a dance. Again in the buses which go long distances, there is a folding seat which occupies the passage between the seats to avoid anyone standing for long spells. Across the following seat, when in the down position in the passage way, is a belt which supports the back and this belt is not permanently fixed at either end and could quite easily be purloined.

Big circular mirrors are in position at all crossroads to allow drivers of vehicles to see the on-coming traffic from any road. These mirrors are not broken, as they recently have been at Rosyth. Other road safety measures are the construction of wide footpaths at both sides of the main roads and this is going on everywhere in the Tatras region on the big scale. The big buses and big lorries, as well as small cars, must carry direction signs for use when turning which are about 18 inches long and are illuminated and are waved furiously up and down. There is very little chance of not knowing that a vehicle is turning right or left. There is not the volume of traffic in this country, but the pre-war roads are narrow and there are large numbers of excellent level crossings. On one journey of about sixty minutes we were stopped about six times to allow trains to pass. And we were in a modern speedy car.

The people of Czechoslovakia have, naturally, many difficult problems to solve, but they have already established a Social Security System which provides for the needs of pensioners and children. This with a high level of wages and no deductions from the pay of the workers. The family allowances are graded so as to rise for each additional child in the family and the old age disability pensions are much higher than in this country.

Their Local Government bodies are frequently re-elected and are divided into regions, districts and local committees, eliminating the waste, confusion and friction caused by our system of large intermingling large burghs, small burghs and landward areas. These local bodies are responsible in their area for all the functions of the National Assembly such as culture, education, housing, industry and so on.

Apart from these matters Czechoslovakia has many attractions. There are the most wonderful caves in Slovakia, in which are grown stalactites and lea pillars. There are great mountain ranges. Many of these mountains have well made winding paths for the climber. Fast moving rivers on which are held international sculling competitions. Health spas, swimming pools and magnificent hotels everywhere. The local committee are maintaining in best possible conditions the many cathedrals, castles and museums. The fabulous wealth of paintings and carvings of these places has to be seen to be believed. Some day, warships will be used to take people to see the wonders and friendly people of other lands, but meantime, those who can ought to visit Czechoslovakia.

Bob Selkirk, 1st August 1957.

A letter to Mary Docherty (15th June 1957)

Hotel Dobass
TATKANSKA
LOMNICA
Czechoslovakia
15th June 1957

Dear Mary,

I expected a letter from someone before now. I have written a thousand P.C's and letter, but no one has come here.

I am having a very good holiday and at the same time learning much. Everything I have seen here confirms our Socialist beliefs, and other ideas.

I have a letter from a Czechoslovakian child for Michael. They want more addresses for school children. Possibly Michael could get some more.

I have bought a few presents but now wonder about the Customs because I have one for each of the grandchildren and that may seem a lot to Customs Officers. I hope all are well at home and that you are not missing Frances too much, not to speak of Michael.

I have been on a visit to wonderful caves, mountain peaks, to sanatoriums, to collective farms and to pubs. There is reconstruction going on everywhere.

I have spoken to the children at school and got very friendly reception from teachers and children. On our delegation are good men comrades and the delegations from other countries are most comradely. I have not yet got any chance of using my Russian, but may yet get a chance to show off.

All the very best,
Yours sincerely,
Bob Selkirk.

The first visit to Russia (September 1961)

3rd September 1961: Visited Permanent Exhibition.

Exhibition shows every phase of Soviet Union activities, scientific, cultural, Industrial progress. Scientific mainly devoted to great advances in physics, medicine etc., etc. First rockets recovered from outer space, wonderful exhibition! Models of sputniks and space ships on show. Greatest interest provoked by Southern and Asiatic Pavilions. Progress most marked by Asiatic Republics, starting from scratch in 1917. These Republics now are most advanced industrial countries. Millions of Soviet people visited the exhibition, composed of Pavilions for each of fifteen Republics, and have seen evidence of wisdom of party leadership.

Visited Lenin University.

Twenty thousand students from sixty countries. A city within a city....(sorry, word I couldn't recognise). Cinemas, shops, laundries etc., within building with playfields on grounds. Magnificent buildings in magnificent situations. Well laid out grounds extending over many acres. Roadways adorned with trees, shrubs, flowers, statues of leading Soviet writers, of artists on roadways leading to University and facilities have been named in memory of world famous persons. Views from Lenin Halls include Moscow River, a sports stadium holding one hundred thousand persons. Cathedrals, Kremlin Towers and blocks of new flats, stretching for mile after mile. Everywhere we went we found thousands of workers in the streets, in the parks, in the magnificent swimming pool, all looking happy and cheerful.

Humanity passing through a critical period.

Transition from Capitalism to Socialism, success of S.U., making Imperialism desperate. Hoping to destroy Socialism by war using West German Fascists as spearheads. Recently, Soviet Government decided to start Nuclear Tests. Communists and other countries support this decision. Communists in Scotland live in a country with American Bases. We know Soviet Union must destroy these bases if war comes. This means death to us, but we declare the Socialist world must be preserved at all costs. Wise policy to let the two German States meet to discuss West Berlin. Imperialists refuse. They want Fascists established throughout the world.

Monopoly breeds Fascism. Fascism breeds war and Colonialism. War brings ruin and destruction to mankind. Soviet Union fights for peace and Socialism. If war comes we must destroy monopoly, capitalism, colonialism, exploitation of man by man. Soviet Union proposes total disarmament. Imperialists want international tension. Soviet Union has taken the correct decision in the interests of humanity.

4th September 1961

I went for my second thorough examination at hospital. In the afternoon I stood as Guard of Honour beside the coffin of William Foster, great American leader. Really moving spectacle to watch the long queues of Russian workers, men and women, waiting to pay their last respects to a great working class fighter. Beside the resting place of Comrade Foster the Moscow Orchestra played appropriate and beautiful music. Red Army soldiers stood guard and acted as stewards, maintaining orderly Changing of the Guard and disciplined marching of queues of workers. I last took part in similar ceremony in 1928 for Bill Heywood, American working class leader.

5th September 1961.

Present at funeral of William Foster, great American party leader, Delegates amounting to thousands of people from factories, shops, offices, Local Government and Communist Parties. Delegations of several hundred from several Brother Parties, India, Brazil, Canada, Cuba, Britain and many others. Elizabeth Flynn delivered a great oration. Bob Stewart made an eloquent speech for our party. Secretary of Moscow Soviet and others also spoke and paid tribute to a great Marxist. Red Army Band played moving music and gave a magnificent rendering of the Internationale, while ashes were placed at the Kremlin Wall, near Lenin Mausoleum and last resting place of other famous Communist Leaders. Apart from delegation thousands of workers poured into Red Square in honour of Foster. Ashes to be taken to America at a later date.

SOVIET UNION PRESS:

Every paper which I saw carried the heading WORKERS OF ALL COUNTRIES UNITED. This was the slogan given by Karl Marx. Over a century ago he gave the workers a guiding principle for struggle to end mass poverty, to end mass exploitation of workers by a ruling minority, and this remains the guiding principle of the Soviet Government. Only the most backward workers fail to understand that their insecurity is due to robbery by capitalists, that they should have powerful government which advocates an end to that robbery. Is it possible to get the significance of this across to every worker? If this truth becomes the property of the masses, the end of capitalism is near.

So Russian people do not read foreign literature lies the capitalist press. Forty per cent of authorities quoted in Russian Medical Encyclopedia are from foreign literature. In libraries many books translated from foreign languages are in Russian libraries. More than we can see in the British libraries.

At the Ballet in the Bolshoi Theatre.

Romeo and Juliet was the Ballet. In the Bolshoi Theatre there are six golden tiers of boxes and balconies, spectacular decorations and lighting. Well over one hundred players took part in the Ballet. Scenery was perfect, sparkling and articulate and reproduced the scenes of ancient life with its golden glitter for the rich and rags for the poor. Even the church, clowns and knights were portrayed. Robust dancing on village squares, all outshone by expressive dancing by leading actors and actresses. The most significant feature being the wrapped attention by thousands of very prosperous looking people who filled the huge theatre to the music, dancing and scenes. Altogether a magnificent show and display

Letters to Mary Docherty
Some extracts describing his experiences in Russia

"I return to Moscow on the 27th Sept, visit Kremlin, University, permanent exhibition, Minister for Social Services, a coalfield and, I hope the puppet theatre. The permanent exhibition is a wonderful display of the progress made in Soviet Union."

(Moscow 132 Hotel. 28th September 1961)

"We have been in two factories, visited the magnificent palace of Catherine, the Empress, been through the fortress where Gorki and thousands of other political prisoners were tortured and many executed........I have spoken twice to TV people and once at a Party meeting and a factory meeting........It is only when one is home one gets some understanding of the heroism of the Russian people in the last war."

(Leningrad. 4th July 1967)

"Today I was at a District Soviet and was moved to tears at the wonderful reception I got from the officials of the First of May District Soviet. The most wonderful was the evidence of the great progress made in this city. Everything possible is done for the welfare of the citizens and to draw the citizens into the participation on deciding policy....You will see the wonderful progress made since you were here in 1920–30."

(Volgograd 6th April 1969)

"I am undergoing treatment, injections, tablets, baths, diet etc. as you know. The medical examinations are very thorough here. It is a magnificent place with well laid out grounds, sports grounds, tennis courts etc. There is a Kino, library, dance and concert hall within the building. More food than one can eat. I have a room with bathroom, and have spent most of my time in my room. No Britisher here except me and my Russian will not sustain a conversation."

(Puskina Sanatorium, Moscow. Saturday 9th September 1969)

"I am still in rest home but you can write to me at the above address....I am greatly improved in health under the great skill of doctor but I will have to get full course of injections. My Heath Brown flake stock is exhausted and tobacco here is very light, just burns away. I am sure if Mr Wilson knew he would send me a couple of ounces, but he does not know. I hope your duties as Editor have been carried out timeously. I will severely criticise when I find out mistakes (of some one other than me.)"

(Moscow 132 Hotel. September 1969)

"I intend to try and publish another book when I get back home on the theme 'Defend the Soviet Union'. I am collecting material for it now. I will as usual be looking for assistance from you."

(USSR May 1969)

Branch Bulletin Report on Bob Selkirk's 4th Visit to the Soviet Union

I thank everyone who made it possible for me to pay my fourth visit to the Soviet Union, and I now report back on my impressions of the trip. I thank everyone: members of the Communist Party here and in the Soviet Union, members of the Labour Party, the Co-operative Party, Trade Unions, members of any other party or organisation and others for the support, which has encouraged me to continue taking part in the sacred struggle for social justice and a world free from poverty and the threat of nuclear world war.

My journey

I travelled by train to London. While in London I had long, very useful discussions with, among others Lawrence Daly, now General Secretary of the British Miners' Union; Gordon McLennan from Glasgow, now National Organiser of British Communist Party. I spent one night in London and in the morning a comrade from the Central Office of the Communist Party called at the hotel and accompanied me to Heathrow Airport and kept me company until the BEA jet plane left for Moscow. The plane flew at 900 miles per hour and made the trip in three and a half hours. The time passed pleasantly as a hearty meal and plenty of reading material were provided free for the passengers.

At Moscow

I was met at the airport by Javad A Sharif, a native of the Azerbaijan Soviet Socialist Republic, who speaks fluently in six languages, Aida Sergeevna, a teacher at the Moscow State Foreign Language College and two other comrades whose names I did not catch properly. A car was waiting to take me to the Hotel October where delegates from many lands were staying. They had come to Moscow for the First of May Demonstrations in the Red Square. Very pleasantly began a trip which took me by plane to Volvograd (Stalingrad), over 1000 miles from Moscow. Nowhere, at railway stations or airports during my trip did I need to order a car, buy a ticket, book a room or carry my suitcase. I was met at every stopping place by comrades who did these things for me. A rich person would have bought service but no amount of money could have bought the friendship I enjoyed.

Delegates from 60 countries had arrived for the important International Communist Conference when I left Moscow on 24th May 1969.

May Day Demonstration in Red Square

Here I heard the Prime Minister of one of the most powerful states in the world declare, before hundreds of thousands of his fellow citizens and hundreds of foreign guests, his Government's determination to carry out faithfully a policy based on the principles laid down by their great leader – Lenin. The principles were embodied in the slogans carried by the demonstrators; the principles of...."A world free from poverty, insecurity and war", "A world of friendship between nations", "The ending of the legalised robbery of man by man".

The Cold War lies

The 'Sunday Post' of May 25th carried one of their usual poisonous tales. It printed "rumours" that the Red Army was in a state of mutiny and this was the reason for there being no military display at the First of May Demonstration. Actually the reason was that the ordeal of "standing to attention" from 9.00am. till 5.00pm. had an injurious effect on the health of the leaders and so the ordeal was shortened by 21/2 hours by cutting out the military display and setting a limit to the numbers from any area taking part in the demonstration. Many more would have demonstrated if quotas had not been fixed. Lies are the main weapon of the lackeys of Imperialist warmongers.

Moscow Soviet

One of my first trips in Moscow was to the Chambers of the City Soviet, which guides all the social and industrial activities of this city with 6,700,000 inhabitants. My first very pleasing discovery was that 47 per cent of the 1100 deputies were women and that on the executive women outnumbered men. One could not but feel shame to have to admit that the skill of women as efficient administrators is lost to the community in Scotland.

Real democracy

50 per cent of the deputies are not members of the Communist Party. Any organisation or residential group can nominate a deputy for election. The final selection is made at a joint meeting of the elected representatives of all the organisations nominating a candidate. The deputy is chosen by a ballot vote of all citizens in the area who are over 18 years of age. The deputies continue at work, except for the executive of 24, and each deputy must report regularly to his or her constituents and must fix days in the week when constituents can interview their deputy. The deputy serves for two years and any one over 18 years is eligible for election.

Income from profits

The Soviet gets its income, not from rates, but from the profits made by factories, workshops, shops, theatres, cinemas, transport etc. in its area. The profits from the labour of citizens do not go to swell the fat bank books of individuals as happens in our country.

Moscow Kremlin

One could spend weeks in this "walled city" admiring the art and culture of the past ages: the crowns sparkling with jewels worn by the Czars and Czarinas of times gone forever, the wonderful valuable paintings and statues, the striking architecture of the towers and cathedrals. Each of them are reminders of the time when exploiters of the workers lived idle luxurious lives at the expense of poverty stricken workers, peasants and soldiers.

Lenin's Rooms

On one of my visits to the Kremlin my interpreter and I joined a group of high-ranking Army and Navy officers who were making a tour of the rooms in which Lenin lived and worked during the difficult days of the Revolution. My interpreter had to repeat to me everything the guide was saying about the exhibits. She did this while the guide was speaking and this must have been a distraction to the officers but instead of showing annoyance, they very courteously made way for me at every exhibit to permit me to get close to the guide. I ought not to have been surprised at this friendly behaviour because everywhere Soviet citizens give foreign workers such courtesy. Soviet people really practice the spirit of the grand slogan ... "Workers of the world unite."

The Palace of Congresses

Inside the Kremlin walls has been built a palace for Congresses because the Soviet Government recognises the great importance of discussion in arriving at the truth. The magnificence and size of this building leaves one amazed. It is also used as a theatre.

Culture ... Culture

There are 25 live theatres in Moscow, another two are being built. I did not get the number of cinemas, but one sees them in every part of the city and more are being built. Judging from the films I saw documentary and comedy films are popular favourites.

There are countless amateur groups presenting plays and ballet and from a very early age children form drama and dancing groups.

At the theatres and cinemas "full houses" are the general rule. No one is allowed to enter the hall while the play or film is on and smoking is forbidden but one can smoke in the entrance corridor. In the new theatres one has quite a walk from the front rows to the entrance corridor, but the interval is of longer duration than in this country.

Educational tours

I witnessed a constant stream of groups, many from distant parts of the country, to Lenin's Mausoleum, Museums, Art Galleries, Panoramas, Memorial Parks and Monuments for soldiers who fell in the wars against the bestial fascists and in the resistance to the invading armies of fourteen capitalist states, invading the First Workers' Republic for the purpose of, as Winston Churchill expressed it, "strangle Bolshevism at its birth." Guides are provided for each of these groups and one is compelled to admire the ability of these guides, most of whom are women. Our woman guide explained the facilities at the Lenin University, with its 6,000 students as if she had been many years a student in it.

Recreation

There are three sport stadiums holding 35,000 spectators but one being built will hold 45,000 and it will be roofed. Boating on the Moscow river is a favourite pastime and the large swimming pools are well patronised. Some critics have drawn attention to the large number of small wooden houses in the pleasant country surrounding Moscow but if they had taken the trouble to enquire they would have discovered that these houses are preserved so that they can be used by citizens as holiday and weekend homes. The Pioneer Palaces of Culture have facilities for all sports and the Pioneer camps have the same facilities and are enjoyed by thousands of children.

A football match

At a football match, which I witnessed, the hour before the start of the match was devoted to displays of skill by firemen, physical culture clubs, soldiers, sailors and pioneers. Races were run, including a marathon race and a marathon walk. The marathons finished before the end of the match and a special cheer was given to a 64 year old man who was last, but did finish the course in the marathon walk. Military and Naval bands provided stirring music during the displays.There was no hooliganism among the 35,000 spectators or players.

Social Services

60 per cent of income to the City Soviet is spent on redevelopment. Having been in Moscow in 1928 the great progress made in housing is very evident to me, but even from the time of my visits in 1961 and 1967 the increased number of new housing estates is obvious. All the houses are centrally heated, the factories have been removed to the outskirts of the city and the air is very pure for a large city. The rents are on average 5 per cent of wages. These rents are not enough to meet the cost of repairs but any deficit is met from the income of the Soviet. Automation is increasingly employed to build houses for the rapidly growing population.

Nursery Schools

There are now sufficient nursery schools to cater for every young child in Moscow and schools and colleges and universities are fully staffed and equipped.

Medical Services

All medical services are free and there is no deduction from wages for sickness benefit or pensions. The hospitals and clinics are fully staffed and there is an industrial medical service of a very high prevention of illness standard. It is worth noting that 75% of the doctors are women and judging from my experience they are most skillful and understanding.

Professor Matkovsky

In Moscow I had several discussions with the eminent Soviet historian, Professor Matkovsky. He informed me that he was writing a History of the British Labour Movement and that he had used several extracts from my booklet, 'The Life of a Worker.' Naturally I felt pleased that I had helped even in a small way, but I quote this incident in order to bring out the great difference between the outlook on labour problems of a Soviet historian and that of any capitalist historian. The Soviet historians believe in co-operation for the common good but the others believe in the "rat race."

Volgograd

This city, previously named Stalingrad, was almost completely destroyed by the Fascists in the Second World War. It has now been wholly rebuilt and extended according to modern Soviet ideas, with well designed workers' homes, wide sweeping streets, parks and tree-lined walks. Still preserved are the walls of a factory gutted by the Fascists and the house where the defenders of Stalingrad held the second floor against the Fascists occupying the ground floor. The battle of Stalingrad was one of the most decisive battles of the war, and Hitler's hordes were forced to retreat – as Winston Churchill put it – "The Red Army tore the guts out of the enemy forces."

The citizens of Volgograd have constructed one of the most striking memorial parks to those who died "that we might live." It stretches for miles, with many statues, the work of famous Soviet sculptors. Flowers bloom everywhere, an eternal fire glows and a museum is carefully tended. This park was constructed even when the city was in the course of being rebuilt.

Hydro-Electric Station

The Volga-Don Hydro-Electric Station near Volgograd, once the largest in the world, was built as part of Lenin's Plan for the electrification of the whole country. The amount of concrete used in building it would have laid a motorway 25 metres wide from the Volga river to London. A large sea was formed to give power to the turbines. The difference in level of water on each side of the dam is equal to the height of a two storey house. Seven years after it went into action it had repaid the cost of building it. It is connected with five seas and provides water for extensive irrigation schemes.

Yalta

This city is situated on the Black Sea coast in the Crimea with a fine climate and in the midst of magnificent mountainous scenery. In and near Yalta there are 25 holiday and rest homes. Such homes are numbered in hundreds along this coast. Some were built as palaces for the Czars and Russian nobility, but many were purpose-built after the Revolution, and are so furnished and staffed that thousands of Soviet workers have enjoyed a health restoring holiday in them.

While in Yalta, I had oxygen baths, oxygen inhalations, warm vapour inhalations and a diet of fish, vegetable salads, fruit juice, mineral waters, sour milk etc. under the daily supervision of doctors. One day I paid a visit to a palace built for the last Czar. 1000 workers were employed for 8 years on its construction. It was intended as a residence for the Czar and his lackeys, but today it is occupied by one thousand workers enjoying a well earned rest.

This is the palace in which Stalin, Roosevelt and Churchill met to sign the Yalta Agreement which outlined the plan for future co-operation of the Allied Powers.

Holiday and Rest Home

The rest home at which I was a guest had been purposely built after the Revolution. It had its own picture house, a swimming pool, a dance hall, tennis and basket ball court and tours to places of interest were frequently organised. Pleasure trips on the Black Sea were also very popular. The Home was high on the mountain side and a deep lift to the beaches was available. On the beaches one saw a sight very pleasing to the eye – hundreds of workers sunbathing, reading, conversing, swimming and boating. It was a very satisfactory state of affairs – productive workers enjoying ideal conditions. From the deck of a pleasure steamer one could see similar scenes along the coast of the Black Sea.

Fundamental differences

The Soviet Socialist Government, unlike capitalist governments, is using every means to increase the purchasing power of its citizens.

Women have equal pay and are treated as equals in every sphere of social activity.

The students have full rights to participate in the administration of colleges and universities, unlike the students still fighting for these rights in the capitalist world.

There is no unemployment but adverts for labour are to be seen everywhere.

The strap or cane is not used in any school – a sign of a higher level of civilised conduct.

Citizens are encouraged to write "letters to the editor" and editors must take up every complaint with the appropriate authority.

The Minister of Social Security works through the office of the Trade Unions in paying sickness benefit and pensions to Trade Union members.

Trade Unions are encouraged to draft bills and to make proposals to the Soviets. Decisions of Trade Union Conferences are given serious consideration by the elected deputies (who are members of their respective Trade Union.)

Trade Unions, to allow for close co-operation of these mass organs, usually have their head office in the same building as the Soviets.

The Soviet Government publicise the same slogans as those used by militant workers in this and other countries. Fife and other councils promoted provisional orders to give them power to prosecute militants who whitewashed such slogans on roadways.

The Soviet Government actively supports the World Peace Movement, takes the lead in presenting peace proposals at the United Nations and international conferences. The Warsaw Pact Powers have proposed the simultaneous liquidation of Nato and the Warsaw Pact and keep on pointing out the real danger of nuclear world war and proposing disarmament.

Bob Selkirk

CHAPTER FIFTEEN
VARIATIONS ON MASS MILITANCY

In Fife and in other industrial areas of Scotland, mass militancy reached high levels in 1921 – 1926 – 1928 – 1933 – 1935 – 1943 and 1948. It is very instructive to study the causes of the working class movement reaching the "peaks" of militant activity and descending into the "valleys" of apathy in the intervals between the 'peaks'.

The basic cause of the main activity in 1921 was the contradiction between progress and poverty; the technological advances in industry contrasted with the steadily lessening power of low wages to purchase the necessities of life, wages losing the battle with rising prices and with inflation. Some people think of inflation as a modern problem, but actually, it was inherent in capitalism and accelerated its pace in harmony with the growing pace of the development of monopoly capitalism.

Other causes of mass militancy were war time experiences; disappointments of ex-servicemen at Government failure to give the promise "fit for heroes" to live in; low rates of benefits paid under the provision of the 1911 Unemployment Act.

The miners were angry because of failure to operate the recommendations of the Shanky Commission. Much propaganda had been carried out in the industrial parts of Fife by the Social Democratic Federation, the Socialist Labour Party, Labour Party, Anarchists and other small groups of militants. The traditional allegiances to the Liberal Party were rapidly weakening. Much revolutionary literature had been sold, including the classic published by Charles Kerr & Co in the United States. Much propaganda had been conducted by John McLean, the Clyde deportees and the Hands off Russia Committee.

The situation in the period culminating in 1921 was such that the desire of the coal owners and other employers to reduce wages acted as the detonator for the discontent to explode in a wave of strikes and demonstrations. The 1919 Housing Act giving women the vote and extending the voting rights of men, and other Government moves, of the kind described by Bismark, the German statesman, as "insurance against revolution", encouraged the militants to make more radical demands. In Cowdenbeath this led to later charges against demonstrators and riots. Large contingents of police and soldiers were drafted into the area, shop windows were broken and the looting of food from shops and fields took place.

The fall-off in mass activity followed the failure to win increased wages. Victimisation, evictions of the most active, the mass media treatment of useless struggle and the propaganda of right-wing Labour leaders were the main reasons for this fall-off of mass activity, but the militant workers kept on organising for the next inevitable "peak" in the age-long struggle for social justice

During the earlier part of this period the militants experienced their share of disappointments, among them the collapse of the Triple Alliance of the three big Trade Unions, the Miners, the Railwaymen, and the Transport workers coupled with the anti- working class acts of the 1924 Labour Government. It is to the point to recall that Lord Londonderry boasted of his "victory" in getting the League of Nations to reject a Soviet Union proposal to "ban the use of heavy bombers". The Labour Government carried out Londonderry's policy by being the first Government to use heavy bombers against civilians in Iraq. The Labour Defence Minister was at this time a prominent pacifist during the 1914-1918 War, but he felt no scruples in bombing civilians. These facts clearly illustrate the historical truth that right-wing Labour leaders find it very easy to betray proletarian international unity and the principle of national working class unity.

The militants were encouraged by the growing strength of the National Unemployed Workers' Movement, and the report of a delegation from the Trade Union Congress on their visit to the Soviet Union, in which they affirmed that the workers of the Soviet Union were the ruling class. The activity of the militants increased when, in 1925, they forced the Tory Government to grant a subsidy to the coal industry and

Prime Minister Baldwin provided a rallying cry for the General Strike when he said "The wages of all workers must come down."

The militants, as well as the Government, prepared for the General Strike. Many books and articles in left-wing periodicals agreed that it was proof of the great power of the workers when united in mass action against reactionary forces.

The militancy engendered by the General Strike of 1926, despite the treacherous action of the right-wing leaders in calling off the strike, strengthened the miners' resolve to stay out on strike. The morale was high, strengthened by the active support of the organised unemployed workers in preventing blacklegging, manning the picket lines, assisting in maintaining soup kitchens etc.

The ability to organise was shown by the widespread forming of Councils of Action during the General Strike and the continuing Miners' Strike. These Councils guided all strike activities and were excellent as examples of an united front and militancy of all workers, despite the harsh repressive measures of the coal owners and other pillars of the establishment. This was shown in many ways, most strikingly by the victories gained in the Miners' Union elections in 1928, when campaigns used the slogan VOTE FOR THE COMMUNIST INTERNATIONAL: VOTE FOR THE COMMUNIST NOMINEE.

The miners voted overwhelmingly for the Communist International and showed, as nothing else could, the high level of political understanding. Under the circumstances, as would be expected, the membership of the Communist Party, the Young Communist League and the Young Pioneers increased greatly. A May Day school holiday and the feeding of necessitous school children were among the benefits won by a school strike, demonstrations and marches.

1927–1935

Very quickly the political scene changes, due mainly to the effects of economic crises of world capitalism, the anti-working class policy of the 1929 Labour Government and the 1931 Labour-Tory Coalition Government. In 1927 Lochgelly had a left-wing majority on the Town Council. In 1929 the Pioneers celebrated their victories by holding a large May Day Demonstration in Lochgelly Public Park, but in 1932 I was sacked by a Tory majority on Lochgelly Town Council for the "crime" of taking May Day off work to appear at a May Day Demonstration.

Jack Leckie had an enthusiastic reception when he spoke at the above mentioned Pioneer Demonstration. Later the same year, in the General Election he only received 1,712 votes against W. Watson's 15,293 votes. This low vote came after sweeping victories for militants in Union and Local Authority Elections in 1928.

In 1931 because of the American dictated cuts in unemployment benefit scales, in Naval wages and the wages of other Government employees carried out by the Coalition Government, mass activity again developed widely. The Invergordon Mutiny, the unemployed marches and protests by Labour controlled local councils forced the Government to resign. This mass activity continued to develop and was expressed particularly in the intensification of unemployed campaigns for work schemes and higher rates of benefit, the formation of united front committees and unofficial strikes. In 1935 W. Gallacher was elected to Parliament and several militants were elected to Councils and to positions in th branches of Trade Unions. This militant mood was shown in many parts of the country. For instance, in 1935 the Durham Miners' Union carried their banner with photographs of Marx, Engels and Lenin on all their demonstrations. The huge expenditure on armaments in preparation for war lessened the number of unemployed, gave steadier employment to many, and this tended to dampen down the militancy temporarily.

1935–1951

Despite the decreases in the number of workers unemployed, inspiring hunger marches were organised to Glasgow in 1935 and to Dundee in 1936. They were just as strongly supported by Trades Councils, the Co-operative Movement and the rank and file workers as the London march in 1932, the Edinburgh march in 1933 and the local marches to Cupar and Kirkcaldy.

In the '30s there was a developing anti-fascist movement against Mosley's gang and when Franco gained power after his victory in the Spanish Civil War there were great manifestations of international solidarity by the militant workers of this country. Franco was helped to victory not only by Hitler and Mussolini but by the supposedly anti-fascist governments in the capitalist world.

Militant workers organised the International Brigade to help the Spanish anti-fascists to put up armed resistance to Franco and his allies. Many militants volunteered for the International Brigade and many made the supreme sacrifice. Franco won the battle but these militants gave us a noble, inspiring example of martyrdom for the ideal of social justice.

An instinctive anti-capitalist consciousness was shown in Fife by the numerous Council and Trade Union positions won by militants in the postwar period and by the forming of new Communist Party branches. As the torrent of "cold war" lies increased in volume and in a more widespread and organised manner many Council and Trade Union positions and Gallacher's parliamentary seat were lost.

Of course, the "cold war" lies were not the only factors causing these setbacks. The anti-working class policy of the Labour Government and the disastrous results of co-operating with the imperialist governments instead of with the left-wing workers' groups were also factors which played into the hands of the right-wing Labour leaders and the Tories.

1951–1973

The fact that Tory Government spokesmen can truthfully retort to Labour Opposition criticism of this or that anti-working class legislation, "When you were in power you did likewise" is the basic cause of confusion and apathy in the ranks of the workers. The Tory retort is also true of the Common Market negotiations, the Industrial Relations Act, the Housing Finance Act, prescription charges, restrictions and price of milk for school children, educational economies, etc. etc. The right-wing Trade Union Congress leaders have done their bit to knock down the militant spirit. This is most clearly shown by their attempt to create the notion that "talks" between the General Council and the Tory Government can change the Tory policy towards the working class and can stop the Tory Government helping "land sharks," property companies, money lenders and other rich parasites.

These right-wingers in the Labour and Trade Union movement refuse to draw a sensible conclusion from the creation of unemployed masses, the deliberate destruction of food, the expenditure on suicidal atom bombs and other weapons of destruction in order to increase the profits of international monopolies. The sensible conclusion is that the capitalist system must be eliminated and only mass action, not talks between leaders, can do this urgent task.

Despite such silly leadership recent events demonstrate the inevitable and growing desire to organise action against the parasitic criminals who support crazy capitalism. The Pentonville Five released from prison, the wave of "sit ins" started by the UCS workers, the miners' strike and the action of many civil servants all point in the direction of militancy and to the time when workers in capitalist countries, developing countries, colonial territories and socialist lands will unite to sweep reactionary capitalism from the face of the earth.

CHAPTER SIXTEEN
LOCAL COUNCIL CAMPAIGNING

To the Editor, The Advertiser, 29.12.67
Dear Sir,

The recent letter in your paper, written by Mr E. Garvie, drew attention to the fears concerning the future of the "Central Workshops". As the letter said, the run down of the mining industry and the closure of the Michael Pit seriously reduces the demand on the resources of the workshops, our only large factory within the Burgh boundaries. Before the organisation of the Fife N.C.B. workshops similar fears were being expressed. At that time much support was expressed for the proposal that the other nationalised industries ought to place their orders for repairs or replacements with the central workshops. Undoubtedly, if the Gas Board, Electricity Board, Railways and Public Transport were to do so, there would be no fear of the rundown or closure of the shops where we have a skilled labour force second to none in the country. It can be said truthfully that the skilled workers in the shops have adapted themselves to all the changes required of them because of the mechanisation of coal production and the changes in production. Changes in the production methods, if any were required, to supply the needs of the other nationalised industries or services would be taken in their stride by the people employed in the shops. It will be a very severe blow to this area if we permit, for lack of campaigning, the rundown of our only factory. It might be argued, as was done previously, that the N.C.B. could hand the workshops over to private industry. However, the empty factories in Old Perth Road should kill this idea.

The same energy put into the suggested campaign, as was put previously into campaigns, to save the workshops can win the sensible demand that is proposed above and so prevent the calamity of being

with no factory in Cowdenbeath and no industry capable of giving the correct training in engineering to our youth, resulting in the wholesale drift of our young folk from the town and surrounding areas.
Yours sincerely,
Councillor Robert Selkirk.

Red Bailie accuses Minister

Mr Selkirk, nominated by Labour Party members for his bailieship said, "We are working with Labour Members on the Town Council but we do not hold meetings to decide policy. It is simply a question of both sides building socialist views".

After being attacked from the pulpit a magistrate said yesterday, "I challenge the Minister to a public debate". Bailie Robert Selkirk makes no bones about being a communist and yesterday when told that the Reverend David Grieve, Minister of Cairns Church, Cowdenbeath, Fife, had been preaching against his appointment as a magistrate said, "I have every right to be a bailie menace!"

In his sermon Mr Grieve, almost half the age of the seventy two year old magistrate, said, "I have fought shy of speaking of communists in the church, as in a sense it is making propaganda for them, but one cannot but feel it is high time people realised how great a menace communism is. In our town a man who is a communist is sitting in the office of a magistrate to dispense justice and has taken an oath of faithfulness to his office. His purpose as a communist is to undermine the institution by which his office is retained and maintained. It is high time the ordinary people clearly understand the threat this consists to society".

Bailie Selkirk, one of two communist members of Cowdenbeath Town Council, said, "I think it was rather cowardly of the Minister to say what he did, where he did. I challenge him to a public debate anytime, anywhere. If taking up bailieship required me to take an oath to the Queen I would have done so. As it was I simply affirmed to uphold the duties of my office. We communists are not out to overthrow the monarchy by force, we are out to have it replaced by constitutional methods. I can dispense justice just as well as any other baillie".

Conditioning

One day I was addressing a meeting at Cowdenbeath Labour Exchange. In the course of my speech I mentioned that the Fife Coal Company had dismissed me for the "crime" of taking action to have fresh air brought into a section in which there were large quantities of black damp. When the meeting finished I was approached by a pupil attending the Higher Grade School. I was shocked at his comment on the above mentioned incident. He said "The coal company was justified in giving you the sack."

I said to him, "Does that mean that you think we should have our lives ruined by breathing in black damp in order to make profit for the coal company."

He replied, "Yes, the coal owner has his money invested in the pit."

I asked him, "Do you think that the coal owner's money is more important than the health of the workers?"

He replied, "Yes, if it was not for the coal owner's money the men would not get work."

I was shocked, but on reflection realised that this was a striking example of how our children are being conditioned to act as submissives to producers of profit.

Communist Councillors

A year or so after Davie Fairlie and I were elected to Cowdenbeath Town Council in 1936, an I.L.P. Councillor admittedly testified to the fact that communist Councillors do make a change for the better in Council administration.

Councillor Miller at a meeting of the Council suddenly got up on his feet and explained, "There is no pleasure in being a Councillor since the communists became members. Nowadays, if a ratepayer cuts his finger, the Council is blamed for it." This explanation was good evidence proving that the Local Council previously to the return of the communists to the Council had not accepted their responsibilities for the welfare of the ratepayer. During the same meeting Bailie Maxwell complained that too many ratepayers' grievances are now being discussed at great length. This led Council Provost Drylie to say, "We must remember Bob Selkirk is the watchdog for the workers."

I can remember at a further Council Meeting when I first raised the need for seats in the High Street that Provost Paterson ruled that putting seats in the street was illegal. I drew his attention to the fact that there were seats in Princess Street, Edinburgh. However, the Standing Orders said that the Provost's ruling was final and I didn't get the majority for the suspension of Standing Orders. The matter had to rest there. Of course I kept raising the matter and automatically seats were put in the High Street and other places throughout the town. They were undoubtedly much used in good weather and much appreciated by elderly persons and harassed housewives.

Fairlie and I found that at Finance Committee Meetings the actual accounts, invoices and so on, were circulated and each member had to examine a hundred or so bits of paper. We immediately proposed that a list be duplicated giving details of accounts, to be posted to each Councillor along with the agenda for the meeting. This gave each Councillor time to thoroughly consider each of these accounts and the reasons for the related expenditure. We also found that the Council representatives to the County Council never made any report to the County Council for their activities or attitudes to the Council business. We fought for and finally got agreement that these representatives report at every monthly meeting of the Finance Committee and the Town Council would advise as to how they should act at County Council Meetings.

N.U.W.M.

One day at the Labour Exchange I was approached by an angry worker. This worker was a "gaffer" on the surface of a local pit. He had been criticised severely in our "Unemployed Bulletin" for his bullying attitude to the men in his squad. He rushed towards me, literally foaming at the mouth and shouting at the pitch of his voice, "I will drag you up and down the street and the police will not interfere with me for doing so." However, he didn't try to carry out his threat and a few months afterwards when he was unemployed he approached me to represent him at a court of Referees and ever afterwards was a firm supporter of the N.U.W.M. – that's the worker's unemployed association.

Experience in the Parish Office

The N.U.W.M. Committee was informed that a sick man living in the Donibristle Rows had been refused "parish relief" by the parish clerk. Mr Sharp of Aberdour (Parish Officer), William O'Neil and I were instructed to go to Aberdour and request that the sick man should be paid. There was no money for fares, so we walked to Aberdour. On entering the Parish office Mr Sharp picked up the telephone and called the police. This was before a single word had been spoken. The police arrived. We told them our business and to our surprise they withdrew. Mr Sharp, without any further conversation, opened his till and gave us the relief to take to the sick man. This was an unusual procedure. Usually, a messenger would have been sent with the money or a relative would have been told to collect it. On the way back Willie O'Neil kept us cheerful describing in great detail a meal a millionaire had once given him in Dublin. That did not help to allay the pangs of hunger.

Another incident was in a Dunfermline Parish Office. I was confident that I was succeeding in persuading Mr Douglas, the parish clerk, to grant my request for relief in a particular case when suddenly over my shoulder came a clenched fist, which landed on Mr Douglas' nose. The fist belonged to J. Haxton, who had accompanied me and was standing behind me. His feelings had got the better of his judgement.

Police

Inspector Buchan of Cowdenbeath proved to be quite the opposite of Inspector Clark of Lochgelly. He seemed to understand that working class agitators had sound reasons for organising campaigns for social justice.

During the 1931 General Election the word went round that the local Tories had booked up all the local halls in order to prevent the Labour Candidate having meetings. It was decided to stop the Tories holding meetings.

A Tory meeting was advertised for the Palais de Dance. We attended in big numbers and when the chairman tried to open the meeting we drowned him out by shouting in unison. The police started arresting some of the people who were shouting and when chairs were being used to defend the shouters I went up to Inspector Buchan and said,

"You are making a mess of this meeting". He immediately said, "You are to blame not me but if you withdraw your people from the meeting, I will free the people arrested". I got up on a chair and asked our supporters to withdraw in order to get our people out of the police cells. We formed up outside and marched up to the police station and the prisoners were immediately set free.

We marched back to the hall and met the Tories coming out and gave them a hostile reception. If this had happened in Lochgelly there would have been mass arrests.

When the General Manager of the Fife Coal Company was planting a tree to commemorate the coronation of King George, the present Queen's father, in a strip of ground at the Parish Church, the unemployed, led by their uniformed flute band, prevented the General Manager's speech being heard. The flute band and sometimes a loud hailer kept up the volume of opposing sounds throughout the royal ceremony. Some of the policemen made a show of arresting some of the ringleaders but they were stopped by Inspector Buchan.

There were eviction protest meetings held whenever an eviction was being carried out in Cowdenbeath, Hill of Beath, Bowhill and other places but only in Lochgelly were arrests made. In some cases the crime was aggravated by the furniture being put back into the house but no arrests were made.

Inspector Clark's predecessor in Lochgelly, Inspector White, was the only Inspector who thought it wise to arrest me for questioning about the Moscow Gold Scare even though I was active throughout Fife, Kinross etc.

The Morning Star 1970

News of the Malayan massacres in the Morning Star this morning reminded me of the time when I stood with a team in High Street, Cowdenbeath selling "The Daily Worker" during the British war against the people who had defended Malaya against the Japanese. The wealthy classes had fled or collaborated with the aggressors. The street was very busy, a football match was about to start. Our sellers were concentrating on their jobs in a last minute effort to sell papers to the fans when suddenly I was pushed aside and a voice said, "Get out of my way. I have just come from shooting people like you". The voice belonged to a soldier with a haversack and rifle who had come from the nearby railway station to spend his leave at home. This incident proves that some soldiers at least knew that they were shooting communists and not terrorists.

In all probability this soldier, coming from an area which suffered mass unemployment during his childhood, had failed to understand that only through the efforts of the communists and their allies we were able to secure the feeding of necessitous school children and get higher benefits. He would not know of the part played by the Red Army in the fight against Fascism. Under a Labour Government this proletarian soldier and others like him participated in the shooting of communists and the National Liberation Fighters in Malaya, Greece and Indonesia, places where the profits of the imperialists were threatened. Such facts underestimate the urgent need for the sale of the "Morning Star". There are no short cuts to the aims of changing the policy of the Wilson and any future government.

Some experiences

At one time I was receiving public assistance from Ballingry Parish Council. When I was receiving the money from Mr Lawson, the parish clerk, he said, "I don't see why a fit man like you can't get a job". I told him if he got me a job I would take it. When I went back the next week Mr Lawson said nothing about a job, but I asked him, "What about that job?" He replied, "You must be a terrible character. I asked Mr Moran, the manager at Number 11 pit about a job for you and he said that if he had a hundred jobs he would not give you one."

Another time, while unemployed, I approached J. Watt, gaffer at the Newton Pit and asked him for a job. He said, "Certainly Bob, I will give you a job because I think it is wrong the way that the coal companies have been treating you." I started work at the Newton on "Oncost" and it was clear that I was not expected to work too hard. I was encouraged to take it easy. At that time the Reform Union published a paper called "The Miner". The paper was running a campaign to expose managerial blunders in support of the case for nationalisation. I wrote an article for "The Miner" pointing out a silly mistake made by the Newton Pit

Manager and the setting of a pump. The day following the appearance of "The Miner" containing the article I was transferred to the most arduous job in the pit, drawing biscuit wheeled hutches containing stones. These hutches were filled to the brim and were hauled a considerable distance. I remained on heavy jobs until the pit closed down. Of course J.Watt was not to blame. He had to obey the orders of the coal bosses.

In the 1920s there was a speeding up of the work processes. Possibly this is best shown by an incident which I witnessed in the Newton Pit. The "gaffer" had on his main job been urging the pony drawers to more strenuous efforts to maintain a steady supply of empty hutches to the miners at the coal face. One day a pony drawing a team of empty hutches stopped before it left the bottom to obey "nature's call". This caused the gaffer to scratch his head and shout at the pony, "Dearie, dearie, could you not just have waited until you got the hutches up to the miners?"

At school, before starting work in the pits, I had been much impressed by the teachers continuously explaining the saying, "Honesty is the best policy". I placed too much stress on this when the gaffer came into our workplace and asked me as I was following the hutch, "Have you put a lot of stones away among the coal?" Being honest I answered, "Yes". I thought that was alright, but my father who was digging the coal thought otherwise and expressed this by striking me with the back of his hand across my face. So much for "Honesty being the best policy."

Nearly a riot

During the struggles of the unemployed Pat Devine and Jimmy Ord were arrested, charged with Breach of the Peace and were sentenced to 60 days in jail. In order to show the support of the unemployed in Fife for the actions of Ord and Devine, it was decided to march through the streets of Kirkcaldy where the alleged crime of the jailed comrades was supposed to have taken place. The unemployed flute band led the march along the High Street. The police were out in great numbers obviously looking for a pretext to draw batons. When we were passing the spot where the police had congregated in great numbers, I noticed a member of the band, who had been supplied with a heavy flute, preparing to hit a police sergeant over the head. Luckily, I was in time to grip the flute and so prevent what might have been a serious situation.

Tricky situation

Marching along Argyle Street in Glasgow with hundreds of marchers, I was immediately behind a man who was quite clearly in a pugnacious mood. I noticed him on several occasions trying to trip up one of the police marching alongside him. This would have led to a nasty situation and I was very pleased to be able to get alongside the marcher and between the policeman and the marcher.

Cowdenbeath Health Centre (by Mary Docherty)

Bob Selkirk and Davey Fairley were elected to the Cowdenbeath Town Council in 1935. Among other things raised by the mothers who had children to take to the clinic for their check-up was the unsatisfactory location of the clinic.

The clinic was in a house at the foot of Burgh Road. It was very small with one room for the doctor or nurse and another room for mothers and children. Only a few could be housed at one time. Others had to wait outside in rain, hail or snow.

Bob and Davie got no support from any of the other councillors to get some improvement at the clinic. After a motion had been defeated at a council meeting, it could not be raised again before a given time had elapsed. Bob and Davie raised it as often as they were allowed.

To add support for a new clinic, the women's section of the Cowdenbeath branch of the Communist Party raised it in all other women's organisations of which they were members. They took petitions outside the clinic and in the High Street. They organised conferences and communist councillors raised it at Fife County Council meetings.

The Health Clinic that Bob visualised was one that would be big enough to house all the Cowdenbeath doctors under one roof. It would also house other medical necessities.

Appointments would be made between doctors and patients which would cut out the time wasted in waiting in doctors' surgeries.

During the war years a new clinic was out of the question. In 1946 the Fife County Council agreed to provide money for alterations to the clinic in Burgh Road. Then they decided against it because money was required for housing, drainage, water and a new school for Kirkcaldy. In the meantime, the communist Councillors did not agree on spending money on the old clinic when it would not take much more money to build a new and up-to- date clinic in a more suitable place.

A year or two later it was decided to build the new Health Centre in Broad Street. In 1959 the new Health Centre was opened by Bailie Blamey. At last, the Health Centre that Bob and the Cowdenbeath branch of the Communist Party had fought for, for all those years, had become a reality.

Following the opening of the Health Centre, Bob raised the question of the old age pensioners having their feet attended to by the chiropodist at the clinic. He raised it at the Fife Health Committee. His suggestion that it should be a free service was agreed and it is still free.

All the doctors are under one roof and appointments are made with one's own doctor which saves a lot of time for both doctor and patient.

Thanks to Bob Selkirk and the Cowdenbeath branch of the Communist Party, health centres are now the expected thing in every area up and down the country. A new clinic was opened first, then the Health Centre as Bob had visualised.

Children

Some folks when they reach over 60 and any children they have had are grown up and left home, don't enjoy the company of young children. Not so Bob Selkirk. He always had time for children, no matter what age. He would spend a lot of time with them, talking and listening to what they had to say.

If Bob was on his way home when Broad Street School children were on their way home for Dinner break or the end of the day, children who lived near Bob would run across the street fighting one another to get walking beside him. Their greeting to Bob was "Aye Bob" then each would start talking. When they came to the street where they lived they continued to walking with Bob till they came to the street where Bob lived, they would then say "Cheerio Bob. See Ye".

When some of them grew a little older they would ask Bob if they could go round the doors with leaflets. If at any time he was distributing leaflets in the street where they lived they would walk round with him till he told them it was time for them to go home.

Willie O'Neil and his wife had a daughter, Charlotte, who had to get everything done for her. She was unable to do anything for herself. Willie, a Party member, active in the Unemployed Movement, accompanied Bob many times in fighting on behalf of the unemployed against those in charge.

If Bob went to meet Willie at his house, he always spoke to Charlotte. He used to get two spoons and show Charlotte what to do with the spoons to play "musical spoons" on the arm of the chair she was sitting on. He would try to help her hold the spoons. Whenever Bob went in the room she was in her face would light up and she would try to say "spoons" so as to get Bob to play with the spoons.

That was not so when I went to the house. As soon as she saw me she would make a sound for Nellie, her sister, to do something for her. She knew that I was there to get Nellie out with me on Party work. Nellie always gave "Chatty" (as they called her) a lot of attention. I used to get Nellie to meet me outside her house so as not to upset Chatty.

Bob always had time for children and did not like to see a child being hit by anyone, not even by by their parents. He was quite pleased when the decision was taken to abolish the strap in the schools. The abolition of the strap was one of the demands of our childrens' movement which we had fought for over the years.

Wartime (1)

One night during the 1939-45 war Bob had a visit from a very nervous soldier. He told Bob he was here to ask what he could do. He had been home on leave from the army. I think they called it Draft Leave. His unit was being sent overseas so they all got home to see their relatives. He should have been on his way with his unit, but he got cold feet and did not go. He knew that he was in trouble for not reporting back.

Bob thought that the only thing that would save him was a Medical

Line from his doctor. Bob also told him that if the doctor did give him a medical line he would have to keep quiet about it for the doctor would be in trouble as well. He got his line and Bob had to sign it as witness he had been sick.

After the war was over and the country was back to electing their local Councils – which had not taken place till after the end of the war -, the nervous soldier stood against Bob's Party in the elections. That was his thanks to Bob for saving him from being "shot for desertion".

Wartime (2)

During the 1939-45 war the Government controlled all labour power. Before the war not many married women had a job, other than looking after their husbands and children. If they had children they could work if they could get someone to look after the children, which was mostly done by the grandparents.

One day a girl came to the Party rooms to ask if Bob Selkirk would help her. She was single, had only a part-time job to enable her to look after her semi-invalid mother. She had a letter from the Government directing her into one of the Armed Forces for women, so she would have to leave home. She told Bob she could not leave her mother to look after herself, that was why she only had a part-time job.

She had written and told them her position, but they had not exempted her. He had a talk with her and told her what to do, saying she would likely get a letter for her to put her case before a Tribunal. After she got that letter she was to come back and see him before she went to the Tribunal.

Before she told Bob what she wanted his advice about she said – "I did not vote for you and I am a Catholic. I asked the priest if I could come to you for help". Bob told her he never asked anyone if they voted for him, or their religion. He helped anyone who who came to him the best he could.

When she got the date of the interview she came to see him. Bob went over with her all the questions they were likely to ask and her answers. He told her to come to see him again on the day of the Tribunal. He went over the questions again to make sure she understood everything and told her not to be nervous and think it was he who was asking the questions. She came back to thank him. She had won, so could carry on as she was. She asked him his charge. He said he never took anything from anybody. She put 2/6d (25pence) on the table but he gave her it back and told her any more trouble and she could come again. She thanked him once more.

Doctors

One night, on arriving home from the Party rooms, Bob had just taken off his boots when there was a knock at the door. The door opened and in came Dr Veitch, one of the Cowdenbeath doctors. He said, "Bob, get your coat on and come with me." Bob said, "Why? Where to?" Dr Veitch said, "There's no time. I'll tell you on the way".

Still wondering what it was all about, Bob got his boots and coat on again. The doctor said, "There's a man and his wife and family in Donibristle at this moment in a tent, their only shelter. The man is very seriously ill with pneumonia. I want you to help me put them back into their house (a tied house). The farmer has had them evicted because the man is off sick.

Bob said, "I'll put them back in". Dr Veitch said, "You would be breaking the law and could be put in prison". Bob said he was aware of that and when they came to the house he said, "I'll burst in the door. You help me".

Very quickly they got the door open and had the family back into the house. A fire was lit and a hot water bottle provided for the sick man. Bob told the doctor that he would visit the farmer in the morning and try to get him to let the family stay in the house. Failing that he would get in touch with the County Council to try to get the family some kind of shelter. The farmer was very reluctant to let them stay in the house even though it was in the middle of winter and very cold and wet. I think it was because Bob was fighting for the man and fearing that Bob would give it a lot of publicity in the papers that the farmer said that he would give Bob a week or two to get them shifted. Bob eventually got them shelter even though houses were in great demand all over Fife. The farmer kept harassing the family all the time they remained in the house. The sick man was the man for whom Bob and Willie O'Neil walked to Aberdour Parish Office to get him money when he was first ill. He did not get in touch with Bob or the Workers Unemployed Committee for the family did not think the farmer would throw them out in such cold weather and with nowhere to go but he did.

Donibristle, a small village with only a few houses, is a mile or two from Cowdenbeath. Dr Veitch was the son-in-law of Dr Primmer. Both doctors were very well thought of. They were ready to attend anyone at anytime. It was before the National Health Service come into being. Dr Veitch died very young and a plaque in his memory hangs in the clinic in Cowdenbeath. Dr Primmer wrote a medical thesis in his late 80's.

C.P. Town Council Bulletin – July 1946

The Cowdenbeath branch of the Communist Party take this opportunity of paying public tribute to the memory of Dr Veitch. We know better than most people just how much he did to help those in distress. The evicted, poverty-stricken victims of a rotten system never appealed to Dr Veitch in vain.

We often had occasion to ask him for help to get nourishing food, clothing or shelter for numerous people in the days of mass unemployment and he never refused. Many people are healthier and happier today because of his readiness to come to the assistance of those fighting semi-starvation scales of income drawn up by Tory Government bureaucrats.

We salute the memory of Dr Veitch, a worthy and out-standing member of the medical profession, who sympathised with those in suffering and helped them despite the criticisms of the Pharisees. He indeed "felt his brother's chains".

CHAPTER SEVENTEEN
LOCAL ELECTIONS

Cowdenbeath Town Council Election, Tuesday 6th May 1952

This election gives the opportunity to each elector to pass judgement not only in the way this town is run but also on the policy of the Tory Government. Labour has held a majority on the Town Council for over twenty years and this Tory Government has already been exposed as a rich man's Government, though it has only been in power for a few short months. If we are to be honest with ourselves, we have to admit we are suffering from a Tory Government because the whole Labour Movement did not force Atlee and company to carry out a militant working class policy while in power.

The Communist Party fights all the time for the operation of a militant policy, against the Tory class. If you want such a policy, you ought to vote Communist. A vote for a Communist Candidate in this Town Council Election is a vote for efficient, fair and democratic Local Government and a vote against large scale re-armaments, which is leading inevitably to high prices and world war.

Everyone now realises that the Tory War Budget means many less houses, much less food, less clothing, less hospitals, Health Centres, schools, playing fields etc. It means more unemployment and more poverty. Right-wing Labour don't fight effectively against the budget policy because of their own pre-war economy cut policy while in power. There are Tories and right-wing Labourites in Cowdenbeath.

The Communist policy is the only party which carries a clear-cut policy of fighting for peace pacts, or drastic reduction in the huge expenditure of taxpayers money on armaments, against dictatorship by the American gangsters and against the Tory budgets, because the the Communist Party really fights the profiteers and the warmongers.

The Tory press, the BBC, right-wing Labour leaders keep up a continuous lying campaign against the Communists. Do not be misled, the Communist fight for world peace on the battle of ideals and a desire for high social and cultural standards. Study our policy and you will find that, like you, we are for a strong united working class movement to fight and beat Toryism in all its forms and disguises.

Study our policy with an open mind. Our policy supports a "Five Power Peace Pact" and drastic reduction in armament expenditure. Bringing our lads home from Korea, Malaya, Egypt etc. etc. Increasing the rate of house building by direct labour. Lower rents. Fit central heating of prefabs. Speed up repair of houses. Completion of the provision of garden paths and fences. Proper lighting and surfacing of back courts. Building of a modern Health Clinic in Broad Street. Install new and proper drainage and disposal of sewage. The elimination of public nuisances, e.g., burning bins and flooding. Building an up-to-date school in Cowdenbeath. Provision of adequate playing fields and facilities. The cleaning of all vacant spaces. Erection of bus shelters at busy bus stops, like Broad Street and Perth Road. A ten mile an hour speed limit on all streets. Removal of all blind corners and other dangerous spots.

Study our record and our policy. Give Bob Selkirk support on the Council. Vote Hoey for Third Ward and Mary Docherty for Fourth Ward.

(Issued by William Sharp, Election Agent, Room 7, Victoria Buildings, Cowdenbeath)

The Town Council Election takes place on Thursday first and I am appealing to every one to cast their vote on that day.

This is the most important Election in the history of the working class. It is your duty to vote and no one should fail to do so. As the Communist Candidate for this Ward I want to reply to the statements published by the Labour Candidate in his Election address. He accuses the Communists of being subservient to the dictators of a foreign power. What are the facts? Is it not a fact that the Labour Party are accepting the dictates of America?

America tells Britain where she should buy her wheat, how Britain should spend her American dollars, America orders Britain to send her troops to Malaya, Greece and China to support capitalists and landlords. Who agrees with the occupation of the Yankee Troops in this country? – the Labour Party, not the Communist Party. Do these facts not prove who it is that accepts the dictates from a foreign power?

The Communist Party at all times have carried out a working class policy for improved living conditions, against wage freezing, for relief of rates in the days of unemployment. It was the Communists who fought the Means Test, who organised the unemployed for work schemes, against hunger, Fascism and war. The Communists have never been subservient to the Capitalist class.

It is very noticeable in the Labour Party Election Address they do not mention the rents increase, the erection of garden fences, or relief of rates for the old people. They do not tell the electors that while the cost of building material goes up they sell Town Council property in the form of a shop with fittings for £75. They do not mention these things because they know that their policy on these matters would not get working class support.

They claim in their Address that they are Co-op Party candidates, but it is obvious to everyone that they rely on Tory support and Tory votes to get into the Council. Surely there is something wrong with their policy when bitter Tory opponents of the Co-operative movement supports Co-operative and Labour candidates.

The Labour Councillors voted for rent increases, the Cripps Budget, Atlantic War Pact. They voted against relief of rates for old folk, against Direct Labour, against speedy repairs to old houses.

You should vote for and support a really working class policy – Vote for the Communist Candidates – VOTE COMMUNIST.

The Communist Councillors fought for the erection of garden fences – the Labour Councillors voted against them. Bailie Blamey at the ratepayers meeting insulted the tenants who are asking for garden fences. He said those who were asking for these were the people who would not dig their gardens when they had fences. He said children should be trained to keep out of gardens, but he appears to be unaware that dogs and cats exist in this world. Tenants are entitled to garden

171

fences – fences are paid for when rents are paid. Fences are urgently needed. You should show you want these and other things which are necessary for comfort, happiness and health.

The 1966 Town Council Election was the last time Bob stood as a candidate. The difference in the vote shows how much the Cowdenbeath ratepayers thought of him. He only once lost his seat and that was because of illness. Nobody could defeat him in the 32 elections. In fact many Labour members refused to oppose him.

1965	A Maxwell	Communist	463
	J Blair	Labour	384
1966	R Selkirk	Communist	662
	A McPherson	Labour	253
1968	A Maxwell	Communist	459
	Mrs McKinnon	Independent	185
	J Livingstone	Labour	129
	W Sharp	Communist	442
	A Anderson	Labour	161
	J Guichan	Independent	147
	J McGhee	SNP	97

Dangerous falsification of history

It is well known that if people were familiar with the real history of the country they would adopt a more correct attitude to the parasitic class which exploits and robs them.

Locally we have examples of the falsification of our history. The "Advertiser" is continually reporting prominent misleaders who deal with local history without mentioning mass unemployment and local strikes. For many years, particularly from 1925 until 1936, over three thousand people from the Cowdenbeath district "signed on" at the Labour Exchange. That is to say that over twelve hundred people in this area tried to exist on fifteen shillings per week, per adult and two shillings per week, per child. But according to our historians their mass struggles against starvation are not history.

The unemployed organised deputations, demonstrations and hunger marches to London, Glasgow, Edinburgh, Dundee and Cupar. They fought tenaciously against being forced to undercut wages. They fought against mass evictions and campaigned for free meals and clothing for school children.

Their strikes against starvation and low wages lasting for many months, in many cases ending in riots and jail is not history. The younger generation are not allowed to hear of these heroic efforts of their fathers. They are kept politically in the dark and so do not clearly understand how a small minority of parasites, Tories and right-wing Labour Leaders have and are continuing to increase their profits by starving and prosecuting workers.

Even today the process goes on. The Editor of the "Advertiser" only prints letters that suit him and only prints parts of letters he desires to publish because most people are unaware of his Tory censorship. They think they are getting all the facts of present day happenings. The Tory press each day dictate, suppresses, distorts and falsifies the news. The Council Minutes do not contain any reference to any proposal which does not give a seconder, the order of business is altered in the minutes to create a false impression and so there goes on in this way a dangerous falsification of history. This persuades folk to submit to being dressed up in uniform and sent to murder colonial peoples whose only desire is national independence. It persecutes people to increase production so that a third world war can be organised and persuades people that Communist workers are enemies of the people in this country.

We draw the attention of the ratepayers to the danger that our Council will stop building Council houses on the grounds of high cost. Already some Councils have done so. The last right-wing Labour Government shoved up the cost of houses by refusing to limit the huge profits of the building trade profiteers and by increasing the rate of interest on housing loans from 2% to 3%.

The Churchill Government have shown they are even more sympathetic to the profiteers and they have the rate of interest up to four and a half per.cent. and so housing costs and rents will go up with a bang. Surely the correct working class line is not to stop building but to unite to kick the Churchill Government out of office and return a Government which will take the necessary action to reduce the cost of houses and build many more. Any other link means submission to the Tory plans to drive down the standards of the workers and not only in housing but as a whole.

They do not practice what they preach

It is always very dangerous when public representatives act in a hypocritical manner, and our Labour Councillors are doing so. Not only on the important question of monarchy but also on the question of Direct Labour. They all say they believe in the superiority of direct labour, but when the local Union branch of the building trade workers proposed the use of direct labour to give a better and a cheaper house, the Labour Councillors turned down the proposal. Only the Communist Councillors were in favour. Nationally the Labour Party advocates Direct Labour because experience has shown this gives a much better and cheaper house than can be got by employing private get rich quick contractors. Locally the Labour Party boasts about preaching Direct Labour by their actions and by their words through their Union branches. It is necessary for the Labour and Co-operative Movement to make their representatives carry out what they preach.

The members of the Communist Party have offered for many years to unite against the Tories with the Labour Party in a real fight to carry out a working class policy. It is very dangerous to be dis-united in the face of the Tory enemy. You can forge unity by pressing for a correct policy.

Dangerous developments

We issue this statement to draw the attention of Cowdenbeath ratepayers to certain dangerous facts.. We do so not only in preparation for the May Elections, which give the electors the opportunity to alter anything they do not like in the running of the small town, but also to persuade electors that it is their duty to take note of the national and international policies leading to disaster and to take the appropriate action.

PART FOUR

TESTIMONIALS TO 'A MAN IN A MILLION'
Testimonials to 'Auld Bob'

"It is a cherished and treasured feature of our way of life that from the ranks of ordinary men and women, individuals can emerge who can be trained to legislate and govern. Such a man is Robert Selkirk."

Provost Anderson

CHAPTER EIGHTEEN
OLD MINER READS HIS LIFE STORY IN SOVIET PAPER
by Tom Johnson
(Evening News, December 1970)

Seven Million newspaper readers all over Russia have just read highlights from the life story of an old Fife miner.

Ex-Bailie Robert Selkirk of Cowdenbeath, 83 year-old veteran Communist, knows just what it was said about himself in 'Pravda'. He began to learn the Russian language at the age of 75 and now reads the Moscow paper with fluent ease.

He sees every issue. A woman employee of Radio Moscow, whom he met on his fourth visit to Russia two years ago, sends him the daily paper in batches twice a week.

Surprise

In his home in Terris Place, Cowdenbeath, Bob today said; "It was a complete surprise when I opened the paper the other day and saw my photograph and an article about me. But he knows how the story got there. About six months ago a "Pravda" writer YURI YASNEV, with whom he spent a fortnight on Volgograd (formerly Stalingrad) made a detour through Fife after being on an assignment to Belfast.

He called at ex-Bailie Selkirk's house and for three hours discussed old times and matters of common political interest. Now the man who was given the Freedom of the Burgh of Cowdenbeath in recognition of 32 years as a Communist Councillor has typed out an English translation of the "Pravda" article. It tells of his lifetime working in the local pits, of his short emigration to New Zealand and Australia where he was jailed for defending "free speech". The Fifer, Russians were told has been arrested eight times and jailed thrice for political activities.

Bob Selkirk from Cowdenbeath
From 'Pravda', 15th November 1970. Translated into English by Bob
Selkirk.

Gloomy, smokey Glasgow was left behind, breaking free from its
stony embrace our car moved smoothly on wide, asphalt road towards
Edinburgh. Drizzling rain was falling. Through front, on which window
wiper was creaking, could be seen brownish, rusty coloured sheep, beds
of bright green cabbages, pastures with parallel rows of hay, to be used
for feeding cattle.

Fields now and then unexpectedly yielded place coal pits, factory
buildings and workers' villages. Such is this part of Scotland. It seems
as if there was not one bit of earth that had not been turned over several
times by human hands.

Now in front appears a wide river over which the very last word in
modern bridges has been built. The driver of the car controls the steer-
ing with one hand, while putting the other hand into his pocket for two
shillings and sixpence which is cost of crossing the bridge in a car.
Passing over the bridge, for which the citizens of Edinburgh and
surrounding area will pay for thirty years or more, we turn North
towards Cowdenbeath, my destination on this journey.

Fellow travellers become friendly on a long road journey, and my
driver accordingly became very sociable. He had time to tell me about
his family, they were Catholics and casually (as if to widen the mental
outlook of a foreigner) he mentioned that which every child learns at
school, the names of Walter Scott, James Watt and Robert Burns. I
responded to his friendliness by informing him that I was travelling to
Cowdenbeath in order to visit a man I had met in the Soviet Union, in
Volgograd.

"Surely he is a rich man, your acquaintance, when you make such a
long journey to see him?" said my puzzled and curious driver. This
question was unexpected. It compelled me to recall Volgograd; the
Square of Fallen Heroes; the Obelisk in memory of the victims of
White Guard terror; the Eternal Fire of the fraternal graves of those
who perished in the Battle of Stalingrad; the changing of the Guard of
Honour organised by the Pioneers of Volgograd. There I met Bob

Selkirk to whom I was now going, thanks to the luck of a journalist forced to spend several days in Scotland. He would go every morning to the Square of Fallen Heroes, sit on a seat in the shade and watch the diverse groups of excursionists, travelling by steamer to Volgograd to stand in solemn silence at these sacred places in this historic city. Afterwards, I witnessed this man, despite extreme old age, refuse to go in a car and walked to the summit of Mamaevka Burial Mound.

Average in height, lean, with prominent brow, framed by grey hair, Bob Selkirk, has good nature and at same time, a sort of gentle shyness. He does not hurry to answer questions, often smiles, and in company tries to remain unnoticed, he does not try to attract attention.

One day at dinner, at which Bob Selkirk was present, in Volgograd, the conversation turned on who, when and in what circumstances those present joined the Communist Party. Someone asked Bob when he joined the Party and he replied that he was a founder member. All at the table were respectfully silent. Before us was a man who personified the history of the British Communist Party.

Someone then asked by whose invitation Bob had travelled to Soviet Union. He replied: "I was a long time Town Councillor in our mining town of Cowdenbeath. When I past 80 years old I decided to retire because of old age. I was asked what I wished to have for a present after these long years as a Councillor. I replied that my dearest wish was to again visit the Soviet Union. A collection was organised among the citizens....and here I am."

Bob was born in 1887 in a small Scottish mining village. At 12 years of age he began to work in a coal mine and spent a total of more than thirty years in pits, as a drawer of wagons, repairer and hewer of coal. From 1911 to 1914 he worked in mines in Australia and New Zealand, where he hoped to find a better life. In the Australian town of Woollongong, at the time of a meeting in "Defence of Free Speech" he was arrested and sentenced to one month in jail. This was his first arrest, but during his life he was arrested eight times and sent to prison three times.

In 1924 Bob was elected secretary of the Party in Cowdenbeath and from that time carried on Party activity. He took part in the "Hunger Marches" of the unemployed workers, and many miners' strikes, in the

"Hands off Russia Movement, in the struggle to defend the Spanish Republic, against the growing threat of Fascism and Chamberlain's encouragement of Hitler. In a few words, Bob was always there where the front line of the British Communist Party was situated.

The Scottish Coalowners took advantage of any pretext to get rid of "trouble-makers" and Selkirk was often forced to change his place of work and for 12 years remained on the 'black list' without a job.

Finishing school with only a primary education, he supplemented his schooling by reading a large number of books.

"Our region of Fife was always know for the militancy of the workers," said Bob, "we often had visits from Harry Pollitt and William Gallacher. Under their influence was formed and strengthened my conviction, my belief in Socialism, in the Soviet Union."

Bob, on his own, without a teacher, studied the Russian language, and can read papers and journals in the Russian language. "The stimulus to study the Russian language came from my journey to Moscow as a delegate to Sixth World Congress. The overwhelming thirst of the Soviet Workers and peasants produced on me then a great impression. It was then the idea came to me so that I could read Lenin in the original."

"Bob, when were you first elected to Council?" asked one of the company. He replied, "In 1935". He was asked, "As a Communist?" and he replied, "Yes, I have always stood as a Communist in elections." Again came this question, "How often were you re-elected?" and the reply was, "Every three years."

One of the company at dinner then asked, "What did you succeed in doing on the Council?" He replied, "It was necessary to stipulate that city councils in Britain are quite different from your Soviet of Deputies. British Councils have much more limited powers. Despite this fact, we were able at one period to get Council to open a municipal restaurant and arrange for workers to get credit at the local Co-operative Society during strikes. We pressed for money to build a local Health Clinic and Old Folks' flatlets. One of the main problems was the bad housing conditions. During the years, I pressed the Housing Committee to start many new Housing Schemes. Together with these matters, we fought for and succeeded in getting the Council to discuss political questions.

We raised such questions as European Security and American aggression in Vietnam. All these efforts, speaking generally, were supported by the electors."

My friend of Volgograd – Bob Selkirk – was really a rich man. Only it is impossible to measure his riches in money, in pounds sterling and dollars, it is not possible to buy his riches, it is not possible to sell his riches. It is only possible to acquire them by duty, honesty, self-sacrifice of a fighting Communist...his title.....a man to be trusted.

At a garage filling station, at the entrance to Cowdenbeath, I asked for directions to Terris Place. The attendant shrugged his shoulders but did not know. I asked others, but they also did not know. Then I asked where Bob Selkirk lived. The attendant then said, "Why did you not ask that at first, who does not know Bob Selkirk?" and they all began to tell me how to get to his house and requested me "not to forget to give their regards to old Bob."

Terris Place proved to be a small side street on the outskirts of the Town with only a few double storeyed Council houses. Bob was astonished to see his visitors suddenly appearing as if from nowhere. I explained that it had not been possible for me to inform him beforehand. "Never mind about that, this is marvellous" said Bob, "very glad to see you again", It was a small room in which we were received by Bob, the furnishings were modest but comfortable. It felt cold though a fire burned in the grate. A table near the window was covered with papers and books. My attention was attracted to a poster hanging on a wall. It depicted several scenes from the life of Lenin. It had ben published in the year 1927 and its author was the artist M. Sokolov.

The driver of the car sat nearer the fire and rubbed his cold hands. Suddenly he said, "Wonderful really, this man so long Council." Instead of replying I said to him "Look here" and pointed to a document hanging on the wall, alongside the Lenin poster. He read the words "For outstanding service as member of Town Council for 32 years, Bob Selkirk is awarded the title of Honorary Citizen of this Burgh of Cowdenbeath".

"Bob", I said to him, pointing to the document on the wall, "This is a surprise". He smiled and said, "Maybe this is another surprise, a new street in the town has been given my name. All this is done, not as recognition of me personally, but is recognition of my fight for the cause of Socialism."

Bob then told us that in the Party Branch Bulletin, he had given an account of all he saw and learnt about the Soviet Union at the time of his recent visit. He added, "From the first days of the October Revolution, the Soviet Union was for me a source of inspiration. I think of the words of Dimitrov about the necessity to defend the Soviet Union from attack, no matter from where it comes, applies with equal force today. Without this proletarian internationalism becomes an empty phrase. With the defence of the Soviet Union must be linked all day to day activity, especially in celebrating the Lenin Centenary. The more I read Lenin, the more striking becomes the profound nature of his thought. In order to write his short article on 'English Pacificisim and Dislike of Theory' Lenin read all the voluminous books of Sidney Webb on Trade Unions."

Bob took part in the publication of the Party Bulletin, carried out much active work for the Scottish Old Age Pensioners, while not neglecting the Town Council work.

As he took farewell of us he presented me with his brief autobiography "THE LIFE OF A WORKER". At the door we met a comrade from London to see Bob about matters connected with the 50th anniversary of the British Communist Party; he said farewell to departing guests and at the same time received other guests. Passing several blocks of Council houses I said to the driver' "....and we have not seen the street named after a living Scottish Communist" and he replied, "But we are already in that street....this is Selkirk Avenue."

YURI YASNEV (Pravda Correspondent.........Cowdenbeath – Moscow)

Peoples Councillor *(by Bob Macilone, 1965)*

Nine year-old Bobby Selkirk, grandson of Bailie Bob Selkirk of Cowdenbeath asked his grandad to get goalposts, swings and chute for the playpark. The reply was, "Son, if you want me to do anything on the Council about it go and get a petition signed." So, Bobby went down with a petition and enrolled supporters. What Bobby did not know was that his grandfather was forging yet another link in the chain that binds five generations of Selkirks who have struggle in their bones, which have grown hard and unbreakable as the parasitical classes they have had to contend with have grown soft. Bobby Selkirk's great, great grandfather was thrown into prison in the 1850's for having committed the criminal offence of quitting his job, thus contradicting the Master and Servant Contract.

He was later to display his contempt for all masters by becoming the first Secretary of the Arniston Branch of the Miners Union. Heading down the pit, contention was the meat on the bones of the Selkirks and mining was in their blood. Bailie Selkirk's father was a miner and he himself was working down the pit at the age of twelve. This was in the Stirlingshire village of Slamanan. Bob Selkirk may well have been one of those ragged children with uncombed hair, who lived in houses almost without furniture and where floors were simply soft clay as described in Tom Johnson's "The History of the Working Classes in Scotland".

With struggle came the idea of Socialism. Bailie Selkirk's father was a staunch Liberal follower of the Scot, Gladstone, whose picture hung on the kitchen wall. He became Lib/Lab and finally took the path to Socialism after being scunnered on reading what another Scot had written in a book about our noble families, also written by Tom Johnson. For Bob Selkirk, Socialism was virtually all out of the coal face. He heard the word for the first time when someone in the pit asked his Dad how he was getting on. His reply came, words intersperse with vicious swings of the pick at a two foot seam, "We'll never get on until we get Socialism." Young Selkirk set off early on the broad road to Socialism. At sixteen he had his first letter published on the theme of an International Union for Miners. At seventeen he joined the Edinburgh S.L.P. and was a member of Arniston/Mid Lothian Branch of the International Workers of the World.

When the family moved from the Lothians to Cowdenbeath he helped to form a group to promote a Communist bookshop in the year 1916. Out of work he moved back to the Lothians and joined the formation branch of Tranent Communist Party. The old simple and clear precepts of pioneering days are still alive to Bailie Selkirk. At the age of seventy eight he carries them around like a banner with all the verve and agility of a man of forty.

Thirty seven years ago he was elected to Fife Education Committee. As organiser of the unemployed movement he fought hundreds of cases and was arrested eight times for resisting evictions and speaking at Labour Exchanges. Now in 1965 he celebrates thirty years on the Cowdenbeath Town Council, which he entered in 1935.

Nothing is too good, too big or too small, if it adds to the welfare of his beloved community. Among his achievements; the adoption by the Town Council of central heating in Council houses; his victory after fifteen years pressure in securing a quarterly meeting of ratepayers, at which Councillors report back; the formation of a Direct Labour Department to build and maintain houses. If anything, he is more enthusiastic over the seats he caused to be provided at advantageous points in the streets for tired citizens to sit and chat, and the houses placed near their stations for policemen and ambulancemen, or the covering he helped to get for the Old Mens' shelter.

Bailie Selkirk has few recreational hours. He finds his relaxation in being Secretary of the Scottish Old Age Pensioners Association.

Ex-Provost Anderson's Testimonial

I have much pleasure in expressing my views on Bob Selkirk. He was one who believed in the Socialist and Co-operative philosophy. Many Labour supporters expressed admiration for the work that ex-Bailie Selkirk did.

The community are very conscious of what they owe to Bob Selkirk, more so the electors of Ward 4 in which he served as their Councillor for 32 years, also a founder member of the O.A.P.

I was elected to the Council in 1961. Although our policy differed from Bob, he was well liked and respected so much the Labour Council honoured him to represent Cowdenbeath Council at Fife County Council, in which he was well respected.

Dinner

ON THE OCCASION OF THE
PRESENTATION OF
THE FREEDOM OF THE BURGH
TO
Ex-Bailie ROBERT SELKIRK

COMMERCIAL HOTEL

on

Wednesday, 19th February, 1969

Chairman: Provost WILLIAM G. ANDERSON

A photograph taken at a Co-operative Conference in 1967.

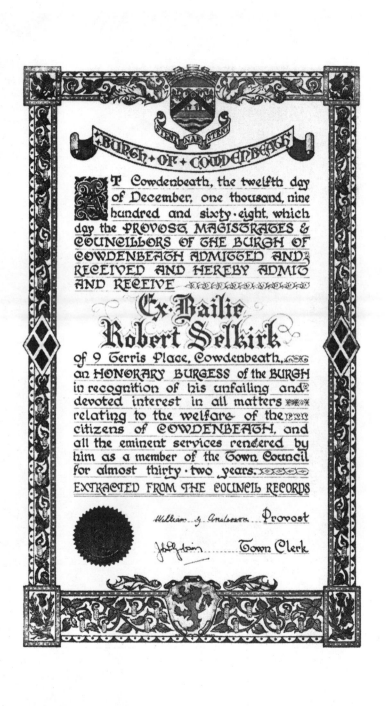

BURGH · OF · COWDENBEATH

AT Cowdenbeath, the twelfth day of December, one thousand, nine hundred and sixty·eight, which day the PROVOST, MAGISTRATES & COUNCILLORS OF THE BURGH OF COWDENBEATH ADMITTED AND RECEIVED AND HEREBY ADMIT AND RECEIVE

Ex·Bailie
Robert Selkirk

of 9 Terris Place, Cowdenbeath, an HONORARY BURGESS of the BURGH in recognition of his unfailing and devoted interest in all matters relating to the welfare of the citizens of COWDENBEATH, and all the eminent services rendered by him as a member of the Town Council for almost thirty·two years.

EXTRACTED FROM THE COUNCIL RECORDS

William G. Anderson .... Provost

John Syme .... Town Clerk

Provost Anderson presenting the Casket to Ex-Bailie Selkirk

*Bob paying tribute to Mary Docherty's parents
on the occasion of their Golden Wedding.*

Campbell would indeed argue bitterly over issues, but Bob seemed always to be in command, and we sat at the "fount of knowledge". Later too I began to question some of his concepts, not in any hostile way, but it did take some time before I realised he wasn't always right, but understandably his ideas had been shaped in a particular period of history, and time and events had moved on. But certainly in the Party Branch and indeed in the town he was held in reverence.

It is impossible to walk down the street with Bob and hope to get somewhere quickly. At regular intervals on the High Street, you would be stopped by somebody with a complaint or seeking advice. Before the days of the Citizens Advice Bureau and the Right Office, he was a one-man Consultant and Advocate for the ordinary folk – the peoples' "penny-lawyer", and he taught me to keep up with Social Welfare Rights and Council Rules and information.

We were the first group to set up our own Councillors Surgeries, in Victoria Buildings and then at our School Street premises, where we dealt with dozens of cases.

Bob was sometimes Machiavellian in his approaches – a wily customer. I remember when I was intending to stand for the Council for the first time in 1964, he got me to take a housing survey of the old houses in the Park Street area. So I went around all those doors talking to the tenants, noting down all their problems of dampness, poor toilets, crumbling walls and so on, and then getting them to sign a petition calling on the Council to re-develop the area. I went about my task with vigour, and eventually the petition was presented to the Council along with the supporting evidence. The controlling Labour group were none too pleased but it was a master stroke in the Council Election campaign and I was returned to the Council at my first attempt, to join Bob and Willie Sharp and give Ward 4 total Communist representation.

Later I suspected that Bob knew before I took the petition that the Council had already planned the redevelopment of the Park Street area, and best all I had done was to accelerate the process. Probably Bob took the view that "the end justified the means", and it certainly was a tactic he employed on other occasions – a little Machiavellian, but of course harmless.

He certainly knew how to use the press, and apart from the regular flow of letters from his pen in the local press, we would arrange wherever possible to have a reporter, complete with camera, when we had a particular issue to pursue.

One such case was when we were calling for the piping of the burn behind Arthur Place, one of his long running campaigns. Bob heard of some sightings of rats in the vicinity, and Willie and I were summoned to appear for a Press photograph looking into the burn, and it appeared under the title of "The Pied Piper of Cowdenbeath". All good stuff and it worked – the burn was piped shortly afterwards.

When I became a Councillor and joined Bob in the Council Chamber I was quickly blooded. Before my first meeting he asked me to sign a paper, without giving me time to read it. Obviously as it was my first meeting I was a bit reluctant to dive in too quickly. However I was horrified to hear the Town Clerk announce at the end of the meeting that a motion had been presented in my name to be debated at the next meeting calling for the "establishment of cervical cancer screening facilities in the Blamey Clinic". That meant I had to propose the motion and reply to the debate at the end – and I knew nothing about the subject!.

I complained to Bob about taking advantage of my inexperience in the Council and told him I knew nothing about Cervical cancer. His reply was, "Well, you've got a month to find out" and he walked away. Over the next few weeks I wrote to all the organisations who specialised in that area, learned all about it and duly presented the motion at the next meeting, with success. The motion was carried, I had undertaken an educational experience, and the facilities were provided. I look back on that incident as an essential part of my training, but I never let him do it to me again without consultation.

That was Bob's way teaching – sink or swim. Another ploy he used to indulge in was also effective. Willie Sharp, Bob and I used to meet prior to Council meetings to agree our 'line' and to decide who would ask what questions in the meeting. Not that we always needed to do that, as in general we would arrive at the same conclusion about issues, given we had the same political and philosophical approach to life.

Willie Sharp normally had a fairly quiet, calm manner during the conduct of Council meetings. However, at an early stage in my Council career I was dumfounded by the attitude Bob was taking at a particular

pre-Council discussion. He was going out of his way to needle and upset Willie, who became angry. He stormed across the Council Chamber and when the issue which had caused the argument came up, Willie rose to his feet like a lion and wiped the floor with the opposition, making a wonderful statement in the process.

Going down the road that night I chided Bob about the incident and again there was a pawky smile across his face as he said, "Well, it worked didn't it". He knew that Willie would perform at peak form if he was upset, and I saw him use that tactic on a number of occasions, although I resisted it myself when I became Group Leader.

He adopted a different ploy with me on numerous occasions. Concerned about a particular Council matter I would go and see him at his home, which was just round the corner from me. I would express my view on the issue to him, and he would give me his opinion. I can well remember in my early days when this happened and we strongly disagreed. He outlined his views and the thinking behind them. I took the completely opposite view and explained why, but I could not convince him, no matter how I tried. Eventually I conceded to his greater wisdom and agreed to follow his "line" in the Council meeting.

In due course the issue came up, and Bob rose slowly to he feet, "Provost" said he, "My colleagues and I have given the most serious consideration to this question and we are of the firm view that...." he then went on to outline to my total astonishment, exactly the opposite to what he had persuaded me to support, and in fact exactly what had been my opinion!.

Again I confronted him later and once more the pawky smile and comment, "Well I have the liberty to change my mind – you were so persuasive!". I remember saying to myself, "You crafty old bugger".

Bob was the master of the Council Chamber. When he rose to speak there was a reverential hush, an acknowledgement of wisdom and respect. As I didn't know him in his younger days, I never saw him as a public orator in the agitational sense, but he had a quick brain and wiliness. On numerous occasions I sat in the Council Chamber as we debated some issue or other and I would think to myself, "They've got you now Bob" only to watch with admiration as he escaped the trap with skill and wit.

He was of course a steadfast supporter of the Soviet Union, no matter what. I can remember in 1968 when the Soviet troops entered Czechoslovakia, to world-wide condemnation. We had a Council meeting that night and as we mounted the staircase the Town Chamberlain, Eric Maxwell called out, "I suppose you'll be 100% behind the Russians, Bob". Bob's reply was instantaneous, "No, not 100%" then a pause, "not 100% Eric – 200%". He remained a champion of the Soviet Union till the day he died, and I am sure he would have been very distressed by events in the last decade.

In spite of those events I can understand the reluctance of people like Bob (and indeed my own parents) to give ground on their defence of the Soviet Union. People like Bob were a product of a particular period in history when the vision of Socialism inspired them to great sacrifice in the fight for social justice, and the emergence of the Soviet Union was to them the living example of Socialism at work. Perhaps it is better that they did not live to see the collapse of the system they had defended so vigorously.

I will look back on Bob Selkirk as a great local figure, a man who devoted his life to the working people. I think there was a streak of the anarchist in him, but again that was a product of his early days. He had a fine mind, a logical way of thinking and could explain complex matters in language you could understand.

If I was to suggest a weakness it would be that he rarely seemed to be involved in anything other than politics, certainly in the time I knew him. Football or other sports had no interest for him, and I cannot recall him talking about social life – dancing, theatre, music. Perhaps he thought these things a waste of time – I never knew.

To me his life was devoted entirely to the fight for social justice. Like Communists of his day it was, "All for the Cause", but I remember him with pride and affection, and it was my honour to give the oration at his funeral, which was attended by numerous major figures in political, trade union and Council circles. He was indeed a remarkable man – local legend and folk hero, and today people still look back with great admiration of "Auld Bob Selkirk".

(23rd March 1995)

84th birthday greetings

Fife Area Committee
Communist Party,
4. 6. 72.

Dear Bob,

I'm writing on behalf of Fife Area Committee somewhat belatedly, but never the less sincere, to congratulate you on the occasion of your 84th birthday. We express to you our appreciation of your life long service to the Communist movement and to the working class, and wish you many more years to witness, appreciate, and give guidance to the struggle and the advances on which I'm sure we're on the threshold of.

Inspired by you example, and comrades like you, we pledge to grasp the new opportunities afforded by the growing desire for change and the new militant mood of the workers, to advance the cause of Socialism.

Best wishes,
Yours Fraternally,
Donald McAulay
SECRETARY

There was time for singing and poetry with a political message. The Young Communist League memorised the following poems and songs at an early age.

POEMS   THE LOWER CLASSES

We plough and sow, we're so very low
that we delve in the dirty clay.
Till we bless the plain with the golden grain
and the vale with the fragrant hay.
Our place we know, we're so very very low
'tis down at the landlords' feet.
We're not too low the grain to grow
but to low the bread to eat.

                THE FLAG

Here's to the flag that's honest and clean,
off with your hats and cheer.
It has braved for many a dismal year
the idiots jib and jeer.
It's the only banner in all the world
that floats o'er a cause that's just.
The reign of right, the end of might,
the doom of the gold-god's lust.

SONGS   THE FLAG OF FREEDOM

Raise high the flag of freedom
in every land and clime.
O'er mine and workshops place it,
an ensign for all time.
Have courage in your action,
fear not the cowardly foe.
Raise high your crimson banner,
strike hard with every blow.

CHORUS   *Then raise the flag of freedom,*
a tribute to our dead.
To all our fallen brothers
who for us fought and bled.
Hark, hark, for they are calling
on us to clear the way,
for workers and for freedom
the dawn of brighter days.

Bob Selkirks favourite song was the "REBEL SONG", reproduced here as an appropriate epitaph to his life-long work on behalf of all workers.

THE REBEL SONG

1) Come workers sing a rebel song,
a song of love and hate,
of love unto the lowly
of hatred to the great.
The great who trod our fathers down,
who steal our childrens' bread,
whose hand of greed are stretched to rob
the living and the dead.

2) Out of the depths of misery
we march with hearts aflame
with wrath unto the rulers false
who wreck our manhoods' name.
The slave who breaks the tyrant's rod
may bend forgiving knee,
the slave who breaks his slavery's chain,
a wrathful man must be.

4) We'll sing no more of wailing
and no song of sighs or tears.
High our hopes and stout our hearts
and banished all our fears.
Our flag is raised above us
so that all the world may see,
'tis the workers' faith and the workers' might
alone can workers free

CHORUS

Then sing a rebel song
as we proudly sweep along
to end the age-long tyranny
that makes for human tears.
Our march is nearer done
with each setting of the sun
and the tyrant's might is passing
with the passing of the years

3) Our army marches onward
with its face toward the dawn
in trust secure in that one thing
the slave may lean upon
the might within the arm of him
who knowing freedom's worth,
strikes home to banish tyranny
from off the face of earth.

THE INTERNATIONAL

Arise ye starvelings, from you slumber,
arise ye criminals of want,
for reason in revolt now thunders
and at last ends the age of cant.
Now away with all superstitions,
servile masses, arise, arise.
We'll change forthwith the old conditions
and spurn the dust to win the prize.

CHORUS

Then comrade come rally
and the last fight let us face,
The International unites the human race.
Then comrades come rally
and the last fight let us face.
The International unites the human race

EPILOGUE

Now that you have read this book, I hope you will agree with me, that Bob Selkirk and the record of his work done on behalf of the working-class deserves to be placed in the annals of working-class history. I trust that this book does just that.

In conclusion, if I may answer a minor criticism written by Alex Maxwell about Bob's lack of social life. Bob enjoyed all of the entertainment he had during his visits to the Soviet Union. At home in Cowdenbeath he did not have the money for socialising and always had some Party work that needed to be done.

I am sure he would have been very glad to know that Nelson Mandela is President of South Africa and would wish him a long life and success in overcoming all the obstacles that will be put in his way.

Mary Docherty
July 1996